SACRED HEAD, NOW WOUNDED

Library of Congress Cataloging-in-Publication Data

Sacred head, now wounded : Resources for Lent-Easter preaching and worship / Daniel Gard . . . [et al.].

   p. cm.

 ISBN 978-0-7586-1485-8

 1. Lenten sermons. 2. Easter—Sermons. 3. Lutheran Church—Missouri Synod—Sermons. 4. Lent—Liturgy—Texts. 5. Easter service—Texts. 6. Lutheran Church—Missouri Synod—Liturgy—Texts. I. Gard, Daniel. II. Title.

 BV4277.R42 2009

 251'.62—dc22

                                             2008044112

1 2 3 4 5 6 7 8 9 10   18 17 16 15 14 13 12 11 10 09

Sacred Head, Now Wounded

Resources for Lent–Easter Preaching and Worship

Daniel Gard

William Weedon

Carol Albrecht

Randy K. Asburry

D. Richard Stuckwisch

CONCORDIA PUBLISHING HOUSE · SAINT LOUIS

CONTENTS

INTRODUCTION

The themes for Lent 2009 derive from the great hymn "O Sacred Head, Now Wounded" (*LSB* 450 [seven stanzas]; *Lutheran Worship* 113 [six stanzas]; *The Lutheran Hymnal* 172 [ten stanzas]). Stanzas of this hymn are cited throughout the sermons.

The sermon texts have been selected to coordinate with whatever lectionary a parish is currently using. For example, the texts for Ash Wednesday and Good Friday are the Old Testament lessons appointed for those days in almost every lectionary series. The text for Maundy Thursday is a unique selection for this Lenten series. The Easter Sunday text is from the Gospel according to St. John, the Holy Gospel appointed for Easter Sunrise in most lectionaries.

The sermon texts for the midweek services, while drawn from Matthew's Gospel, are consistent with Parts I–V of the conflation of the Gospel accounts of the Passion found in *Lutheran Service Book: Altar Book* (pp. 487–500).

TEXTS AND THEMES

ASH WEDNESDAY

Theme/Title: A Wounded Savior for a Wounded People
Text: Joel 2:12–19

LENT MIDWEEK 2

Theme/Title: The Wound of Betrayal
Text: Matthew 26:20–25 (The Passion of Our Lord Jesus Christ: I. The Lord's Supper)

LENT MIDWEEK 3

Theme/Title: The Wound of Apathy
Text: Matthew 26:36–45 (The Passion of Our Lord Jesus Christ: II. Gethsemane)

LENT MIDWEEK 4

Theme/Title: The Wound of Denial
Text: Matthew 26:69–75 (The Passion of Our Lord Jesus Christ: III. The Palace of the High Priest)

LENT MIDWEEK 5

Theme/Title: The Wound of Mockery
Text: Matthew 27:27–31 (The Passion of Our Lord Jesus Christ: IV. The Praetorium)

LENT MIDWEEK 6

Theme/Title: The Wound of Abandonment
Text: Matthew 27:45–48 (The Passion of Our Lord Jesus Christ: V. Calvary)

MAUNDY THURSDAY

Theme/Title: A Meal for the Wounded
Text: Exodus 24:3–11

GOOD FRIDAY

Theme/Title: The Wounds That Heal
Text: Isaiah 53:1–6

EASTER SUNDAY

Theme/Title: He is Risen! The Wound of Death Is Vanquished!
Text: John 20:11–16

SERMONS

Ash Wednesday

A WOUNDED SAVIOR FOR A WOUNDED PEOPLE

JOEL 2:12–19

TEXT

"Yet even now," declares the LORD, "return to Me with all your heart, with fasting, with weeping, and with mourning; and rend your hearts and not your garments." Return to the LORD your God, for He is gracious and merciful, slow to anger, and abounding in steadfast love; and He relents over disaster. Who knows whether He will not turn and relent, and leave a blessing behind Him, a grain offering and a drink offering for the LORD your God?

Blow the trumpet in Zion; consecrate a fast; call a solemn assembly; gather the people. Consecrate the congregation; assemble the elders; gather the children, even nursing infants. Let the bridegroom leave his room, and the bride her chamber.

Between the vestibule and the altar let the priests, the ministers of the LORD, weep and say, "Spare your people, O LORD, and make not Your heritage a reproach, a byword among the nations. Why should they say among the peoples, 'Where is their God?'"

Then the LORD became jealous for His land and had pity on His people. The LORD answered and said to His people, "Behold, I am sending to you grain, wine, and oil, and you will be satisfied; and I will no more make you a reproach among the nations." (Joel 2:12–19)

SERMON: A WOUNDED SAVIOR FOR A WOUNDED PEOPLE

We heard it at the start of today's liturgy: dust you are, and to dust you shall return. The ashes for which this day is named show no one that you are fasting—for who knows if you are?—but they do show everyone that you are dying, and of that you and everyone else may be sure. Dust we are, and to dust we return. Such is the wages of sin.

But then we stare in amazement tonight at One for whom those words sound so wrong. We see Him and cry out: "O sacred Head, now wounded, With grief and shame weighed down, Now scornfully surrounded With thorns, Thine only crown!" (*LSB* 450:1). If ever there were a head that did not call for the ashes of this day, it is His sacred head! Why thorns, when it should be a golden diadem? Here we see in our flesh the One who formed us from the dust at the first. Here is the One who in unfathomable love for our fallen race became dust for us. And now He will even lay down His head into the dust? But there is no sin in Him! In Him, there could be no death. How and why will He die? We will spend all this Lent pondering in awe such questions.

When Joel declares a sacred fast, when he urges the trumpet to sound and the people to gather, we discover that the occasion is one of return. Lent is always about a return *to*. We so often think of it in terms of turning away *from*—what we are giving up, what we will fast from. Make no mistake about it: it is a good thing to fast. Did not our Lord assume that His disciples would do so when He said in tonight's Gospel: "when you fast"? *When*, not *if*! But by itself fasting, going hungry, can be nothing more than an empty religious exercise. The Lenten fast goes deeper than your decision to deny yourself some tasty treat. Rather, it invites, it summons, it urges you back to *someone*, to the Lord. "Return *to* the LORD your God, for He is gracious and merciful, slow to anger, and abounding in steadfast love; and He relents over disaster" (Joel 2:13). A Lent that is anything less than a return in faith to the Lord is only a religious game and worth less than nothing.

Rather than play games with God, hear in this sacred season His summons to you to come back to Him, to return to Him now. He does not want some piece of you, some outward display, torn garments and such, a few minutes tossed His way one day a week. No. He wants *you*, your heart. Hence, rend your hearts!

"A broken and contrite heart, O God, You will not despise" (Psalm 51:17). A heart that is rent, torn open, is a heart that is wounded, damaged, broken. Such a heart God receives from you as a pleasing sacrifice. When, from the depths of your being, you plead, "O God, have mercy on me, a sinner! I have made such a mess of it all. I have hurt so many people and failed so often to show Your love, and You know how terrible my thoughts and how soiled my desires are with sin. Have mercy on me, O Lord! Have mercy!"

Lent is not for pretend sinners. Lent is for real, honest-to-God sinners who have failed in their love of God, who have failed in their love of neighbor, who see this reality, and who by God's grace despise their sin and ache for His forgiveness and for strength to do better. To such the invitation rings out as sheer refreshment: "Even you, even now: Return!" Return, and see the sacred head of Your Savior now wounded. *This* is the One we are summoned to return to. He is the One who knew that we, on our own, could not come to Him, return to Him, find Him; so He came to us, returned to us, and found us.

And we marvel this Lent at how far He went to find us. For it is a marvel indeed that the God of Israel, Yahweh, should take on flesh and blood—as He did in the incarnation. That is enough to leave us astounded forever. But He went further. Not only did He take on our flesh and blood, not only did He become dust for us, but He also went so far as to lift off from us the burden of our sin, to bear it in His own body to death, to own all our failures to live in love as His very own. Indeed, in the words of St. Paul: "He, who knew no sin," became sin for us "so that in Him we might become the righteousness of God" (2 Corinthians 5:21). He not only died, but He also died as the greatest sinner of all time, with the sin of the world upon Him—all of it. Yours. Mine. Everyone's. Thus the Lord revealed that He is indeed merciful and gracious, slow to anger, and abounding in steadfast love. Look to the cross and see! He bore your sin to death that neither death nor sin might be the end of you. Such is the measure of His love.

During Lent, when the Church calls us to return, she is calling us to return to Christ, to draw near to this Savior who was wounded for our transgressions, who was bruised for our iniquity, upon whom was the punishment that brought us peace, and in whose stripes we find healing. She reminds us that the only real life in this whole world is fellowship with Him, communion with Him, and that every time we have settled for anything less, we have allowed ourselves to be deceived and cheated of the great gift of which Baptism made us heirs.

As often as she sets the Table, the Church calls for all her children to return, to come to this wounded Savior who bore our wounds in His own flesh, spilling His blood for us, so that His flesh might be our living bread from heaven and His blood the blotting out of our every sin.

Dust we are, and to dust we shall return, and so the ashes. But the shape of the cross recalls that we have a Savior who became dust for us, whose sacred head was laid in the dust of death that the dust of our corrupted being might be rendered incorruptible in Him. Is it any wonder that, pondering such love, the Church raises her voice to that sacred Head and joys to call it her very own, her greatest treasure?

Midweek 2

THE WOUND OF BETRAYAL

MATTHEW 26:20–25

[The Passion of Our Lord Jesus Christ: I. The Lord's Supper]

TEXT

When it was evening, He reclined at table with the twelve. And as they were eating, He said, "Truly, I say to you, one of you will betray Me." And they were very sorrowful and began to say to Him one after another, "Is it I, Lord?" He answered, "He who has dipped his hand in the dish with Me will betray Me. The Son of Man goes as it is written of Him, but woe to that man by whom the Son of Man is betrayed! It would have been better for that man if he had not been born." Judas, who would betray Him, answered, "Is it I, Rabbi?" He said to him, "You have said so." (Matthew 26:20–25)

SERMON: THE WOUND OF BETRAYAL

The "sore abuse and scorn" that paled our Lord's head "with anguish" (*LSB* 450.2) began long before the physical abuse. It began with the actions of a friend, of one whom He loved, a companion with whom He had traveled many miles and shared many meals. Here was a wound that weighed down our Lord's sacred head and brought Him sorrow and grief that compounded the weight of sin He bore upon His cross.

"One of you will betray Me," He said at the table that night. And they became sad and asked one after another, "Is it I, Lord?" We, too, need to ask that question of our Lord: Have I sold You out, Lord? Have I lived for this world and its pleasures and bought into them, rather than wanting You, spending time with You, hearing Your words of life? Have I lived as if I mattered most and You mattered not at all? Is it I, Lord?

Jesus makes it clear: the wound of betrayal is not inflicted upon Him by those who are distant from Him, from those who are not His companions, His friends, His close ones. No. This is a pain that comes from those nearest to Him, from those whom He held in special love. "He who has dipped his hand in the dish with Me will betray Me" (Matthew 26:23). Not someone distant and unknown, but someone near, dear, loved.

But note the love of the Lord! Do not think for one second that the Lord's love for Judas, His betrayer, was altered by the betrayal. Of our Savior the psalmist spoke truly: "The Lord is good to all, and His mercy is over all that He has made" (Psalm 145:9). He loved this man who would go his senseless way. Jesus loved this man who would first despise and turn from His love, and then despair of what he thought he had lost forever. For Judas, the betrayal was so big a sin that he was convinced he would never find forgiveness. Oh, the betrayal was a horrible sin in Judas, and it is a horrible sin in us. What on earth can justify handing over the Creator of all, who has showed us only benevolence and love, into the agony of torture, crucifixion, and death? What madness is it that would lead the creature to betray the kind Creator? What folly to chase a few bucks for a while in this world, spurning all the while the gift of a life that never ends?

"The Son of Man goes as it is written of Him, but woe to that man by whom the Son of Man is betrayed! It would have been better for that man if he had not been born" (Matthew 26:24). Did our Lord ever utter such a terrifying word? But do you see, people of God, that Jesus did not say these words out of hatred, anger, or any such thing? He spoke from the depth of His sorrowful compassion. He saw, as is His way, where Judas would end his life, that in the end Judas would despair of the mercy of God and go to his grave believing that his sin was stronger than God's mercy in Christ. And it broke our Lord's heart even more than the betrayal itself.

How little Judas understood the Son of Man whom he betrayed! For it was also for the sin of Judas, and the sin of all us Judases, that the Son of Man stretched His hands on the wood and let them pound in the nails. It was for the sin of Judas, and of all us Judases, that the Son of Man pleaded, "Father, forgive!" It was for the sin of Judas, and of all us Judases, that the Lord of life let "grim death, with cruel rigor" (*LSB* 450:2) rob Him of His life so that sin and death would lose their claim over us forever.

The pain of betrayal is great, and it wounded our Lord's tender heart. But it could never turn that heart to bitterness. In that heart lives a love too great, too strong, too mighty for bitterness and hatred to ever conquer it. Although betrayal hurt, and hurt like hell itself, Jesus went on loving—Judas, you, even me.

And so in the wounds of the Crucified One we discover a love that sets us free to love as we have been loved. You know what that means. Our Lord spoke often of taking up our cross and following Him. Do you see, now, what your cross is? You are betrayed when you love, and instead of your love being returned, it is rejected. Such betrayal hurts and wounds you in an unspeakable way, and you are crushed and reduced to tears. Then the old Adam rises up inside in indignation and anger and eagerness to get even. But by the strength of Christ's cross, by the power of your Baptism into His love, you get to nail the old fellow to the wood and say: No! By the power of Him who forgave me, even when I have betrayed Him so many times, I forgive. By the power of Him who loved me, even when I sold Him out, I will love you, the one who has hurt me. This is a cross, my friends. And it will be torture and death to the old Adam, but to the new self that God created in Baptism, it will be joy and life. You will be sharing in the very life of your Savior.

We have not begun to love with Christ's love until we have come, by God's grace, to love those we thought were our friends but who have betrayed us, hurt us, and brought us sorrow. When we go on loving them and seeking good for them and their blessing—a feat impossible for fallen human nature, but possible in communion with the love of Christ—we begin to taste something of the joy known by the martyrs of Christ across many centuries, those who loved and prayed for the people who brought them even to death.

As often as the Church celebrates the Eucharist, she celebrates the love that is in her Savior, which is stronger than all our betrayals—a love that He gives us freely in the body and blood that won forgiveness for Judas, for you, and for all. It is our experience of such love that frees and strengthens us to bear the wounds of betrayal ourselves, following our Lord with joy. May He give us grace to do so, our crucified and risen Lord, to whom be glory with the Father and the Holy Spirit forever and ever!

Midweek 3

THE WOUND OF APATHY

MATTHEW 26:36–45

[The Passion of Our Lord Jesus Christ: II. Gethsemane]

TEXT

Then Jesus went with them to a place called Gethsemane, and He said to His disciples, "Sit here, while I go over there and pray." And taking with Him Peter and the two sons of Zebedee, He began to be sorrowful and troubled. Then He said to them, "My soul is very sorrowful, even to death; remain here, and watch with Me." And going a little farther He fell on His face and prayed, saying, "My Father, if it be possible, let this cup pass from Me; nevertheless, not as I will, but as You will." And He came to the disciples and found them sleeping. And He said to Peter, "So, could you not watch with Me one hour? Watch and pray that you may not enter into temptation. The spirit indeed is willing, but the flesh is weak." Again, for the second time, He went away and prayed, "My Father, if this cannot pass unless I drink it, Your will be done." And again He came and found them sleeping, for their eyes were heavy. So, leaving them again, He went away and prayed for the third time, saying the same words again. Then He came to the disciples and said to them, "Sleep and take your rest later on. See, the hour is at hand, and the Son of Man is betrayed into the hands of sinners." (Matthew 26:36–45)

SERMON: THE WOUND OF APATHY

He did not want to be alone as He wrestled in prayer that night. How often we forget that our blessed Lord was truly and fully human! He needed the comfort of companionship, the encouragement that comes from loved ones. And so, as Jesus leaves the larger group of His disciples behind, He takes with Him His three closest friends: Peter, James, and John. He can no longer keep back the sorrow and the grief that is weighing Him down. "My soul," He says, "is very sorrowful, even to death; remain here, and watch with Me" (Matthew 26:38). He stumbled a few steps further and landed on His face.

Before the eyes of His soul that night was the cup. In order to understand the cup, you must go back to the Old Testament. David sang: "For in the hand of the LORD there is a cup with foaming wine, well mixed, and He pours out from it, and all the wicked of the earth shall drain it down to the dregs" (Psalm 75:8). Isaiah foretold of a time to come when the cup would pass from the people: "Thus says your Lord, the LORD, your God who pleads the cause of His people: 'Behold, I have taken from your hand the cup of staggering; the bowl of My wrath you shall drink no more'" (51:22).

So the cup that was set before our Lord for Him to drink and empty down to the bitterest dregs was the cup that held the wrath of God—the wrath of God against all your rebellions, all your lovelessness, all your passing of judgment upon others, all your selfish acts, all your indulging the flesh, all your spiritual apathy. It was set before Jesus and He saw it. And He knew exactly where it would lead. Jesus quotes from Zechariah: "I [that is, the Lord] will strike the shepherd, and the sheep of the flock will be scattered" (Matthew 26:31). Make no mistake about it: our Lord receives His Passion as entirely from the hands of His Father.

But how He struggled with it! None of us is nearly as frightened of hell as we should be. None of us has the first clue about the real terror of its empty and eternal loneliness. None of us can begin to fathom either its icy coldness or its ever burning and unsatisfied hunger and thirst. But Jesus—the Eternal Word of the Father made flesh of the Virgin—He knows. And before this reality, looking into that ultimate and eternal poison in the cup, He trembles.

He trembles, and He begs the Father that, if possible, some other way may be found, some different approach, something other than what is in this cup before Him. He looks over the brim of the cup into its fathomless depths, and He shakes in terror.

We sin so blithely. "God will forgive," we say. "He is loving and merciful and kind. It is really no big deal." Go with your Lord to Gethsemane tonight, and see with your own eyes whether or not it is a "big deal." Look at Him as He shakes before the very portion that we foolishly choose for ourselves time and again. And see Him, as He lifts His eyes from the cup to His Father and pleads for some other way. But then see our Savior manifest that radical and ultimate difference between Himself and all the other sons of Adam and daughters of Eve. See Him lower His eyes to the cup again and say, "Nevertheless, not My will, but Yours be done."

It has exhausted Him, terrorized Him—looking into that cup. And so He turns back to His friends, His beloved, for the comfort they can give. But here another wound strikes Him. As He has struggled with the terrors of death and hell for them, they have fallen asleep. "Peter!" He cries, startling them awake. "Could you not watch with Me one hour? Watch and pray that you may not enter into temptation. The spirit indeed is willing, but the flesh is weak" (Matthew 26:40–41).

Weak. That is what our flesh is. Weak, and so we wound our Lord with our apathy. We wound Him with our blithe sinning. We add to the terrors of the cup He must drink. Surely Jesus' word of warning will keep His disciples awake and in prayer? The most terrifying events of their discipleship are only moments away now. Surely, they will realize and pray? But no. They are like us after all, or we are like them.

Jesus turns back and again makes the same struggle in prayer. Then He returns for comfort from His friends and again encounters only apathy—they are sound asleep. He is all alone with this. He turns back for His final prayer. The sweat falls from Him in great drops like blood under the pressure of His "yes" to the Father's will. He will do it. He will go forward to drink this cup. He will do so, trusting that, having imbibed the poison of our whole race and experiencing in Himself the penalty of our disobedience, His Father will not abandon Him—the Innocent Sufferer. Look into the face of your Lord as He rises from that final prayer. What do you see now? You see peace.

The peace came from His prayer. The peace came from His trust in the Father. To submit to the One who has loved you with an everlasting love is in the end not terror, but joy—no matter how dark the path. In that peace, Jesus turned back to His disciples for the last time. Their apathy can wound Him no more; He is going forth to swallow it down with all their sins and the sins of the whole world. So while they slept, He won the battle, and He won it alone. He will now go forth to meet His betrayer. He wakes up His disciples from their sleep to meet the terrors to come.

And seeing Him march forth to meet this end in peace, we sing in astonished awe:

> What Thou, my Lord, hast suffered
> Was all for sinner's gain.
> Mine, mine was the transgression,
> But Thine the deadly pain.

Lo, here I fall, my Savior!
'Tis I deserve Thy place.
Look on me with Thy favor,
And grant to me Thy grace. (*LSB* 450:3)

As He looked in pity on the three disciples, so Jesus looks in pity on you and me. And by the struggle of His will to drink the cup and empty it for us forever, He shows us that He will never be apathetic about us. He who drained that cup can be counted on to save us to the uttermost—and to Him be glory with His all-holy Father and the life-giving Spirit, now and unto the ages of ages!

Midweek 4

THE WOUND OF DENIAL

MATTHEW 26:69–75

[The Passion of Our Lord Jesus Christ:
III. The Palace of the High Priest]

TEXT

Now Peter was sitting outside in the courtyard. And a servant girl came up to him and said, "You also were with Jesus the Galilean." But he denied it before them all, saying, "I do not know what you mean." And when he went out to the entrance, another servant girl saw him, and she said to the bystanders, "This man was with Jesus of Nazareth." And again he denied it with an oath: "I do not know the man." After a little while the bystanders came up and said to Peter, "Certainly you too are one of them, for your accent betrays you." Then he began to invoke a curse on himself and to swear, "I do not know the man." And immediately the rooster crowed. And Peter remembered the saying of Jesus, "Before the rooster crows, you will deny Me three times." And he went out and wept bitterly. (Matthew 26:69–75)

SERMON: THE WOUND OF DENIAL

"Even if I must die with You, I will not deny You!" (Matthew 26:35). That is what he said. Peter loved his Lord. He could not imagine the intense love he felt for Jesus ever being insufficient. But the Lord knows what is in man. And in fallen mankind there is fear—fear of death above all. Fear of death, as Hebrews (2:15) puts it, is how the devil keeps us in bondage. So the Lord tells Peter before it ever happens that it will happen. Not once, not twice, but three times Peter will be given opportunity to confess His Lord. And not once, not twice, but three times, Peter will instead deny Him.

Among the wounds that afflicted our Lord during His Passion, surely the denial of His beloved disciple Peter figures large. And who among us has not added to that wound? For opportunities to confess our Savior arise at every hand, yet how often we pass them by in silence. And our silence denies Him. Isn't our fear the same? The fear of the death of others' respect, the fear of the death of their friendship (for who wants to befriend a religious fanatic), the fear of the death of our reputation (for what will others say about us if we are known for speaking up in confession of the Lord)? And so the silence, which is denial just as surely as saying, "I do not know the man."

But see! Jesus goes into His Passion to be wounded for our transgressions. Our denials of Him—they need not result in His denial of us. For He has carried them to death, and where we denied, He made the good confession before the high priest and before Pontius Pilate. Jesus did not let fear of death deter Him, and we do well to ponder that.

For though our Lord hates death—despises it, scorns it—He does not fear it. He came into this world to destroy it. He came among us to let death devour Him, so that by falling into its stinking gullet, the One over whom death had no claim would destroy death forever, and so His people would be set free from their slavery, set free from their fear.

Standing before the high priest, Jesus knows what is about to happen. He knows that He will yield His life upon the cross—a fragrant offering and sacrifice to His Father, His blood blotting out forever the guilt of our sin and the sin of the whole world. And Jesus also knows and rejoices that His Father will never abandon Him to the grave. Although death takes Him, death's bands will be burst. The way several Early Church Fathers put it, Jesus was death's poison pill. Having swallowed Him down—the utterly indigestible Divine Son of God—death began to wretch and ended up vomiting all it had swallowed. Jesus does not fear death, because death will never be the end of Him or of anyone who is joined in living faith to Him.

Now Peter has only heard that Jesus will be raised from the dead, but before his eyes he beholds the Master in the hands of those who are beating Him and who will turn Him over to be crucified. Peter's heart quails, and he trembles and fears. Rather than in peace confessing His Lord, in terror of death Peter denies Him. And as the fateful rooster crows, he recalls how His Lord said it would be so, and Peter goes out and weeps bitterly.

Peter wept bitter tears for his own fear and sin and cowardice, but he did not despair. Here Peter differs from Judas. Did he recall the look in his Lord's eyes when He said, "Remember, I told you that you would deny Me, and I was right, so you have. But remember that I also told you I would rise again, and I will be right about that too! I have prayed for you, Peter, that your faith fails not!"

Now think of the man we meet on the other side of the resurrection, on the Day of Pentecost. The man who cowered before the serving girl and her friends boldly tells the crowds that day: "This Jesus whom *you* murdered by hanging on a tree God has raised from the dead, and we are all His witnesses!" (see Acts 5:30–32). What stands in between? The resurrection of Christ and the coming of the Spirit.

And so it is with you and your Baptism. There in the waters you are placed into the tomb with Christ and raised with Him as the guarantee of a life that will never end. In those waters, the Holy Spirit descended on you even as He descended on Peter and the other apostles on Pentecost, transforming them from quivering cowards to bold confessors. What changed was the conviction of faith that Jesus truly has destroyed death's power by enduring it, and He has atoned for all our denials by His confession and suffering for us.

Years later Peter was told that he had to sacrifice to the emperor and deny this Jesus or die. In the grace of God he refused. He refused, and Peter went the way of his Lord. He, too, was crucified, though, according to Church tradtition, upside down, because he did not feel himself worthy to die in the same manner as the Christ. In the end, Peter looked the fear of death in the face and laughed at it. "You cannot scare me this time! I know who lives forevermore, and I know you have no power over Him. And I am in Him, and His body and His blood are in me. My sins are forgiven, blotted out. My life is secure. You lose, Death, even as you take me. I am not afraid of you—not anymore."

Well might Peter's prayer have been that day what we sing tonight:

> My Shepherd, now receive me;
> My Guardian, own me Thine.
> Great blessings Thou didst give me,
> O Source of gifts divine.
> Thy lips have often fed me
> With words of truth and love;
> Thy Spirit oft hath led me
> To heav'nly joys above. (*LSB* 450:4)

Midweek 5

THE WOUND OF MOCKERY

MATTHEW 27:27–31

[The Passion of Our Lord Jesus Christ: IV. The Praetorium]

TEXT

Then the soldiers of the governor took Jesus into the governor's headquarters, and they gathered the whole battalion before Him. And they stripped Him and put a scarlet robe on Him, and twisting together a crown of thorns, they put it on His head and put a reed in His right hand. And kneeling before Him, they mocked Him, saying, "Hail, King of the Jews!" And they spit on Him and took the reed and struck Him on the head. And when they had mocked Him, they stripped Him of the robe and put His own clothes on Him and led Him away to crucify Him. (Matthew 27:27–31)

SERMON: THE WOUND OF MOCKERY

They thought it was hysterical—this Galilean peasant pretending to be a king. It cracked them up. They decided to have some fun with His apparent delusion, so the soldiers began by taking away His clothes. He had to stand there naked as they mocked Him. Then they found a beautiful scarlet robe and put that around His shoulders. "There. Now He is beginning to look kingly," they joked with one another. "You know what is missing? We need a crown!"

And so one of them thinks up a crown for this peasant king from Galilee, a crown to teach Him a thing or two about His silly daydreams, a crown of entwining thorns. "Thorns and thistles it shall bring forth for you" (Genesis 3:18). They smash the crown down upon His head, and the thorns bite and the blood pours. And still He stands there. His response is not what they had hoped for. He is silent to the taunts, the mockery, the jeers.

Someone comes up with another missing item—a king needs a scepter. They scrounge around and find a reed, and they make His right hand take it. They step back to admire the finished product: blood running down His face from the thorns cruelly piercing His head, His naked body barely covered with the red scarlet robe, and a flimsy reed that flops this way and that in His hand. "Behold, the man who would be king," they say.

Laughing with scorn, they fall on their knees. "Oh, Your majesty!" they cry. "Hail! King of the Jews!" Still He looks on in silence, as their mockery turns vicious. He will not play along in their game, so He will pay. They begin to spit on Him to show their utter contempt of this deluded upstart. They take His scepter and whip His head with the reed. "Some scepter. Some rule. Some kingdom. You are nothing, and You are about to die, and it will not be easy. Wait and see, King of the Jews."

And as He looks on them, what these men miss is the depth of His pity for them, for these who wound Him with mockery, who try to shame Him, and who are preparing to torture and murder Him. Look into His eyes, though, and you will see it—a depth of pity and a fountain of love that will shake you to your core. It is a mere human trait—common to all of fallen humanity—to love your friends and to seek to do them good. But to love your enemies, to have nothing but pity and compassion for those who taunt and jeer at you and who are preparing to kill you—that is the mark of the heavenly Friend, of Jesus Christ.

> What language shall I borrow
> To thank Thee, dearest Friend,
> For this Thy dying sorrow,
> Thy pity without end? (*LSB* 450:5)

Limitless pity—no end to it. The look of pity from the face of the mocked King extends not only to His torturers but also to the entire human race, which is complicit in His death. "Father, forgive them, for they know not what they do," He would say a few hours later (Luke 23:34).

Of course, the truth beyond all truths is that Jesus actually is King—*the* King promised to the Jews. Yes, Jesus is the long-awaited Son of David. But even more, He is the King for the Gentiles and their Ruler. He is the One to whom the entire universe belongs. Every one of us—including those who mocked and shamed Him—owe their existence only to His will that we exist. You will never ponder the Passion aright until you remember that a single thought from Jesus could have undone all those who sought His death, a single thought could have destroyed us all. But in that highest provocation, all He returns is love, pity, mercy. For that is what fills Him. That is who Jesus is. And this is how He reigns as King above all kings: He rules in love unconquerable by hate.

For you see, Jesus is determined to share fully in the lot we have chosen for ourselves. We were destined to sit on thrones of glory and to be robed in majestic garments and to wear crowns on our heads. Such was what our God wanted for us, why He created us in the first place. But we threw it all away and embraced instead the path of suffering and death, of loneliness and pain. He would not have that be our end. He came to walk that path as King so that through His sufferings all that we lost might be restored to us again.

Jesus is stripped, that our sinful nakedness might be clothed in the bright robe of His righteousness. He wears a crown of thorns, that we might wear a royal diadem. He is beaten and mocked, that we might be welcomed and treasured. Love Incarnate will overcome all hatred and mockery and remain Love, that a way would be opened for us to return from this misery of sin and death into the kingdom the Father planned for us from the beginning.

Jesus walks that way—that suffering way—in kingly fashion. None of the mockery can take from Him His majesty, His glory, His peace. He does every act of His Passion in burning love for the fallen race of men so that we might be restored. He chooses to lay down His life that we might live in Him.

Such love on His part begets love on ours. That is why we sing together:

> O make me Thine forever!
> And should I fainting be,
> Lord, let me never, never,
> Outlive my love for Thee. (*LSB* 450:5)

Behold, your King! Behold—beneath the spit, the blood, the blows—the eyes that look upon you with tender compassion and cry out: "For you, child. For love of you. That you might live with Me forever."

Midweek 6

THE WOUND
OF ABANDONMENT

MATTHEW 27:45–48

[The Passion of Our Lord Jesus Christ: V. Calvary]

TEXT

Now from the sixth hour there was darkness over all the land until the ninth hour. And about the ninth hour Jesus cried out with a loud voice, saying, "Eli, Eli, lema sabachthani?" that is, "My God, My God, why have You forsaken Me?" And some of the bystanders, hearing it, said, "This man is calling Elijah." And one of them at once ran and took a sponge, filled it with sour wine, and put it on a reed and gave it to Him to drink. (Matthew 27:45–48)

SERMON: THE WOUND OF ABANDONMENT

How many are the wounds we inflicted upon our Savior in His Passion, suffering, and death! We have pondered together the wounds of betrayal, apathy, denial, and mockery. We have seen ourselves, our own lives, reflected in Judas, the sleepy three, Peter, and the soldiers. Yet of all the wounds that our Lord received, none so struck, so terrorized, and so weighed on Him as the one we ponder tonight. We did not inflict this wound. It came from His Father—the wound of abandonment.

From out of the unspeakable depth of His agony on the cross, our Lord cries the words of Psalm 22: "My God, My God, why have You forsaken Me?" The great Lutheran preacher O. P. Kretzmann ponders this cry of agony:

Suddenly on a Friday afternoon a man was forsaken of God, cut off from the living and the dead, utterly and ultimately alone.

26

The sudden emptiness in those shadowed eyes. . . . It was then, much more than afterward, that He died.

You see, this is sin. It is not merely a matter of murder and adultery and gossip. Something to do or not to do! It is always loneliness. It is cutting yourself off from God. It is a deliberate turning away from truth, from goodness, from heaven.

You see, this is redemption. All this He took into Himself, alone there in the dark. He became sin for us. (*The Pilgrim* [St. Louis: Concordia, 1944], 47)

Dear people loved by God, as all the sin of the world is laid upon the Lamb of God, as He owns it as His very own, He experiences in Himself what every one of those sins demands: "Leave Me alone, God! Go away! Leave Me be!" This is the bitterest dregs of the cup that Jesus will drain down for us in its entirety. He will taste hell. He will taste it for us all. He will know the loneliness so profound that its pain is unimaginable for us. How can we begin to understand what it was like for Him in that moment—the Eternal Word, who had delighted in the Father's presence before the ages came to be; the Eternal Word, who took on flesh from the Virgin without ever leaving the presence of His Father; the Word made flesh, who lived among us constantly, as all men were meant to live: conscious of His Father's never-failing love and the presence of His guiding hand. And all this is now withdrawn, and Jesus is alone. All alone.

People joke about hell, saying, "Well, at least I will have a lot of company there." Wrong. Utterly wrong. Think of the story of Lazarus and the rich man. In that story, the rich man is all alone. Lazarus has angels for company and Abraham, to whom he is so close that he lays his head in his bosom. The rich man hungers and thirsts for a human touch. "Send Lazarus to dip the end of his finger in water and cool my tongue, for I am in anguish in this flame" (Luke 16:24). But no visit relieves the terror of the rich man's solitude. He is alone. All alone. And will be alone forever. Ponder that, and you will begin to understand the reality of hell. Ponder that, and you will see its true terror. Ponder that, and you will bow in love before the Savior whose love for you was so great that He chose to enter that loneliness Himself and to endure it in your place that you might be set free from it forever. Never alone. Never again.

Because Jesus endured the wound of abandonment that our every sin demands of God, because He drained the cup down to this, its last and bitterest dregs, you can look to your Savior and pray with the confidence of being heard:

> My Savior, be Thou near me
> When death is at my door;
> Then let Thy presence cheer me,
> Forsake me nevermore!
> When soul and body languish,
> O leave me not alone,
> But take away mine anguish
> By virtue of Thine own! (*LSB* 450:6)

Do you see it now? You will never have to know what Jesus went through in those darkest hours. You will never have to face life or suffering or death alone. He has made sure of it. He will be with you. He will walk with you every step of the way, and so hell itself is undone, death destroyed, sin forgiven. Your Savior, your Shepherd, He attends you through the valley of the shadow of death so that you fear no evil, for you are not alone, but He is with you. His rod and His staff they comfort you. He brings you out from that darkest of valleys into the sunshine and the bright light of the day that never ends in the kingdom of your Father.

O. P. Kretzmann will have the final words on this meditation on the wound of abandonment:

> Above His "Eli, Eli" was the sound of tearing veils, of falling walls, of the glad crying of those who now had a home again after the long loneliness of sin. They would continue to wander, groping, stumbling, falling, in all the black ways which man will walk when they turn away from God. . . . But there was a way back now, beyond Jerusalem and beyond thought and hope to the place where the open arms of the cross had become the gates of heaven. (*The Pilgrim*, 47)

Maundy Thursday
A Meal
for the Wounded

EXODUS 24:3–11

Text

Moses came and told the people all the words of the Lord and all the rules. And all the people answered with one voice and said, "All the words that the Lord has spoken we will do." And Moses wrote down all the words of the Lord. He rose early in the morning and built an altar at the foot of the mountain, and twelve pillars, according to the twelve tribes of Israel. And he sent young men of the people of Israel, who offered burnt offerings and sacrificed peace offerings of oxen to the Lord. And Moses took half of the blood and put it in basins, and half of the blood he threw against the altar. Then he took the Book of the Covenant and read it in the hearing of the people. And they said, "All that the Lord has spoken we will do, and we will be obedient." And Moses took the blood and threw it on the people and said, "Behold the blood of the covenant that the Lord has made with you in accordance with all these words."

Then Moses and Aaron, Nadab, and Abihu, and seventy of the elders of Israel went up, and they saw the God of Israel. There was under His feet as it were a pavement of sapphire stone, like the very heaven for clearness. And He did not lay His hand on the chief men of the people of Israel; they beheld God, and ate and drank. (Exodus 24:3–11)

Sermon: A Meal for the Wounded

Did they realize, did they have the first clue, what they were agreeing to? "All that the Lord has spoken we will do." We do not need to think about all the Lord had commanded to realize the hopelessness of their response. We can think merely of the two chief commandments, as our Lord gives them from the Law: love the Lord your God with your all, and love your neighbor as yourself. "We will do, and we will be obedient." Really? With your all? And from the depths of your being?

Have you ever tried it? To love God with your all, I mean. Your heart undivided by competing loyalties, but given to God and to Him alone. Your only desire to enjoy His presence and to do His bidding. Your only fear that you will cause Him some displeasure. You go give it a whirl, and let me know how it goes! And then there is your neighbor, the one made in God's own image. Love this one as yourself. Or, again, as our Lord paraphrased, do to others as you want others to do to you. Have you given it a yeoman's try? You most certainly should!

But I am afraid you and I would end up about as successful as the people of Israel who put up the big promise, then promptly fell flat on their faces. Their journey through the wilderness to the Promised Land was hardly characterized by love of God above all and love of neighbor as self. Instead, there was grumbling against God and the way He led them; distrust that He would provide them with water, with food; neighbor squabbling with neighbor and wearing Moses out as he sat on the judgment bench from dawn to dusk to try to settle their petty squabbles. "All that the LORD has spoken we will do, and we will be obedient." Not so much.

So despite their words, despite their foolish trust in themselves and in what they could muster, the covenant was sealed with blood. Part of the blood went on the altar; part, on the people. And with the blood went forgiveness. For there is no remission of sins without the shedding of blood. And it was as blood sprinkled the people that Moses and Aaron, Nadab and Abihu, and seventy elders of Israel climbed the mountain to see the wonder of God's glory. They saw Him, and the beauty wounded their hearts. There He was upon His throne, and at His feet a pavement as of sapphire, blue and crystal clear as the sky above. And in God's presence, as the blood-covered ones, they were able to sit down and to eat, and they did not die, but lived—though they knew they had no right to see such holiness and continue breathing.

They lived despite the fact that they did not keep their end of the covenant. They lived despite the fact that love for God did not characterize their all. They lived despite the fact that they did not love their neighbor as themselves. They lived because they were under the blood, and under that blood the presence of God came to them as an experience of life, not death.

Today is Maundy Thursday. We are well aware that we have failed to keep this covenant of the Lord. The Ten Commandments, which spell out the shape of love in our lives, accuse us without end: No, we do *not* love the Lord with anything close to our all. No, we have *not* loved our neighbors as ourselves. Like Israel of old, we have *not* kept the words of the Lord to do them, no matter how many times we have promised to do better, to change. Yet Jesus still comes to us this night and readies a gift for His people that has been on the heart of God from before time began and that will go on sustaining His own until the day of His glorious appearing. He would provide a meal for His wounded people, His broken people who do not live up to the covenant of love. He would feed them with His own body and blood so that they might live, so that they might be forgiven, healed, and restored.

And do you realize why there is life in *that* body and blood? Because it is the body and blood of the One in whom there was nothing *but* love—love for His Father with all His heart, mind, soul, strength, with His all. And just as surely, there was love for the neighbor, for you and me and for every member of our fallen race. Jesus loved us as Himself, indeed more than Himself. For us He will allow that body to be nailed to the tree and that blood to stain the earth, wiping out the curse of the Law that is against us. You see, the Law can never condemn Him, for His whole being—His every word and thought and action—was always and only love. And He calls us to live under that blood.

To live under that blood is to taste something better than the food Moses and Aaron, Nadab and Abihu, and the other seventy elders of Israel ever knew. We not only eat and drink in the presence of the All-Holy One, but also through our faithful eating and drinking, He—the God of Israel, who appeared in glory to the ancients, who is now made flesh—comes to us, to enter us with His forgiveness, and to plant within a wounded people a life that death cannot overcome. We live because of what He gives us to eat and to drink: the body and the blood of Him who is Love—Love incarnate, Love crucified, Love risen and triumphant and coming in glory.

"A new commandment I give to you, that you love one another: just as I have loved you" (John 13:34). The strength of your love for one another and for Jesus will now always pour into you from this gift of His love for you. His gift in the Eucharist guarantees that what you now enjoy in a hidden and mystical way will be your eternal joy in the life to come. His gift gives you the courage and strength to sing and pray, even as death comes to you:

> Be Thou my consolation,
> My shield, when I must die;

> Remind me of Thy passion
> When my last hour draws nigh.
> Mine eyes shall then behold Thee,
> Upon Thy cross shall dwell,
> My heart by faith enfold Thee,
> Who dieth thus dies well. (*LSB* 450:7)

Enfolded in His cross, marked with the blood of the covenant, fed with the body of Him who is immortal Love, you will be prepared for your passion, suffering, and death whenever it comes. You will be held by a love that is stronger than death and a forgiveness that is greater than all your sin. To Him alone be glory forever—our Lord Jesus, who gives us this meal to heal the wounded with His love.

Good Friday

THE WOUNDS THAT HEAL

ISAIAH 53:1–6

TEXT

Who has believed what he has heard from us? And to whom has the arm of the LORD been revealed? For He grew up before Him like a young plant, and like a root out of dry ground; He had no form or majesty that we should look at Him, and no beauty that we should desire Him. He was despised and rejected by men; a man of sorrows, and acquainted with grief; and as one from whom men hide their faces He was despised, and we esteemed him not.

Surely He has borne our griefs and carried our sorrows; yet we esteemed Him stricken, smitten by God, and afflicted. But He was wounded for our transgressions; He was crushed for our iniquities; upon Him was the chastisement that brought us peace, and with His stripes we are healed. All we like sheep have gone astray; we have turned—every one—to his own way; and the LORD has laid on Him the iniquity of us all. (Isaiah 53:1–6)

SERMON: THE WOUNDS THAT HEAL

We adore You, O Christ, and we bless You, for by Your holy cross, You have redeemed the world. Amen.

Crucifixes make us uncomfortable—and well they should. We squirm before them, and it has nothing to do with any anti-Catholic bias. It is simply painful to look upon our Lord suffering so and to know the reason for His suffering. We shudder before it. We sing:

Mine, mine was the transgression,
But Thine the deadly pain. (*LSB* 450:3)

In the darkness of that Good Friday, the totality of human sin—from the first sin of our first parents to the last sin of the last human being alive—all of it was gathered up, pressed together, and then off-loaded onto this Man. He bore the whole weight of it and owned it as His own. Thus He also bore its penalty—both temporal and eternal death.

Look upon Christ's cross. See His wounds, the nails affixing His hands and feet to the beams. See the blood running down His face from the thorns. Behold the quivering mass of His mutilated back as He is forced to rub it against the tree, pushing up against the nails to take in a breath of air. Look, seek, realize: this wounded Man, dying in agony, is not suffering for a single wrong that He has done. As we have seen, His whole life was only love. He was the only human being who completely loved the Father with His all and His neighbor as Himself. Yet it is because Jesus *is* love that He is now upon the tree. Love will not leave the sinner in his sin. Love takes that sin upon Himself. Love is wounded to grant us healing. He is offering atonement for all the wrongs that *we* have done.

Yes, it is hard to look a crucifix in the face, for it is hard to accept the truth we sing:

> Lo, here I fall, my Savior!
> 'Tis I deserve Thy place. (*LSB* 450:3)

Yet it is salutary to look—salutary to fall on our knees before His bleeding image and to ponder it. It is good even to beg Him to imprint this image on our hearts, so that we might carry it with us wherever we go, so that it can be before our eyes also in the moment of our death. You see, when the moment of your death comes to you, Satan will press hard. In that moment above all, he will seek his last chance to snatch you away from God forever, and he has a powerful weapon to use. The cunning serpent minimizes sin when he would lure you into it with temptations, but then he maximizes your sins in your memory in the hours of despair. When death is coming for you, he will happily set up the DVD player in your mind and replay for you the many sins you have forgotten all about. He will taunt you, then, that you are no Christian. He will declare you unfit for the kingdom of God. He will tell you that you are *his* and that you willed to be his with every sin you committed along the way. And all those sins will be playing all the while in vivid detail and color before your eyes as you are struggling in death.

And that is why it is vital to train yourself in life to look upon the crucifix, to behold your Savior's wounds, and to hold them close to your heart, counting them as your most precious treasure. In the hour of your death, they will be your only weapon against the despair of the enemy You will be able to look at all of your sins as the accuser brings them before your eyes, and you will be able to acknowledge their hideous nature as an irrefutable testimony to your countless failures. But against them all you will set another image: the image Isaiah holds forth for us today—the image of the Crucified One. And it is this image that will shatter the devil's attempts to draw you into despair before your death. Thus we sing:

> Remind me of Thy passion
> When my last hour draws nigh.
> Mine eyes shall then behold Thee,
> Upon Thy cross shall dwell,
> My heart by faith enfold Thee.
> Who dieth thus dies well. (*LSB* 450:7)

The image you want before your eyes as they are closing in death is the image of the Son of God in His last agonies, fully owning and answering for your every sin, pouring out His blood to blot out the accusations of the Law that Satan would use against you. For awful as your sins are, each one has been accounted for, covered over in innocent blood, the blood of your Lamb, your Jesus. "And they have conquered him by the blood of the Lamb and by the word of their testimony" (Revelation 12:11). In that hour, you will say with boldness: "Lord Jesus, you are my righteousness, just as I am your sin. You have taken upon yourself what is mine and have given to me what is yours. You have taken upon yourself what you were not and have given to me what I was not" (AE 48:12).

Thus you indeed will be prepared for death when the image of the Crucified One hangs before your eyes and you know that His life is now your righteousness; His death, your forgiveness; His wounds, your healing; His sufferings, your crown and glory. People, you have been loved by God. God in the flesh, Jesus Christ, has indeed proved your dearest Friend, and He would make you His forever. Look upon His cross boldly, confidently, continually, and you will see.

We adore You, O Christ, and we bless You, for by Your holy cross You have redeemed the world.

Easter Sunday

HE IS RISEN!
THE WOUND OF DEATH IS VANQUISHED!

JOHN 20:11–16

TEXT

But Mary stood weeping outside the tomb, and as she wept she stooped to look into the tomb. And she saw two angels in white, sitting where the body of Jesus had lain, one at the head and one at the feet. They said to her, "Woman, why are you weeping?" She said to them, "They have taken away my Lord, and I do not know where they have laid Him." Having said this, she turned around and saw Jesus standing, but she did not know that it was Jesus. Jesus said to her, "Woman, why are you weeping? Whom are you seeking?" Supposing Him to be the gardener, she said to Him, "Sir, if you have carried Him away, tell me where you have laid Him, and I will take Him away." Jesus said to her, "Mary." She turned and said to Him in Aramaic, "Rabboni!" (which means Teacher). (John 20:11–16)

SERMON:
HE IS RISEN! THE WOUND OF DEATH IS VANQUISHED

It does not matter how many times you encounter it, it never feels natural, never feels right. Death always feels wrong. Something inside does not accept that we will not hear that voice, see that face, touch that hand, experience that laughter ever again. The grief counselors can talk till they are blue in the face about how death is simply a part of life and how we must accept it as inevitable and natural. But we never do. We never will.

Mary did not accept death. Oh, she had no doubt that her Lord, her

Teacher, was dead. She had witnessed the horror of it. Standing beside His mother, she had seen the light die in His eyes as He hung gruesomely upon the cross. She had seen them take His limp body from the wood, heard the horrid sound as they pulled nails. He was dead. She had no doubt of that.

But it was not right. She knew it was not right. And she simply had to touch Him again. It was imperative to her that she *see* that body again. But the body was gone. She had run to tell Peter and John—big help they were. They checked it out and told her she was right: the body was gone. Then they left her, but she remained. She did not know what to do, where to go, to whom to turn. So she just stood there and started to cry.

Not the easy, gentle tears of the merely sad, but Mary wept the gut-wrenching, full-voiced sobs of the grieving. Death. It wounds not only those it takes from us, but it also wounds those who are left. And sometimes it wounds us so badly we think it will kill us then and there. Mary knew something of that as she sobbed and looked into the tomb.

But something was different now. The tomb was not empty after all. There were angels there, clothed in white. One was sitting where the Lord's head had been, one where His feet had been. And though Mary's sorrow could never shake or destroy their joy, they are concerned for her. "Woman," they ask, "why are you weeping?"

Jesus' death was such a given that she did not say, "Because my Lord is dead." Instead, her answer was, "They have taken away my Lord, and I do not know where they have laid Him." Not knowing about the location of the body was tearing her up. Death was horrible enough, but not to be able to find the body? Not to be able to tend it and give it her last services? She *had* to know where Jesus was, to touch His body once more. How else could she face tomorrow? How else could she face the rest of her life?

Mary's grief is of such a magnitude that a conversation with angels does not faze her. So she straightens up and turns and almost runs into the One who had never been far from her, the One who stood right beside her in her grief—though she knew it not. He gently asks, "Woman, why are you weeping? Whom are you seeking?"

Hope rises in Mary's heart. Is it the gardener? Perhaps he is the one who moved her Master's body. "Sir," she cries, "if you have carried Him away, tell me where you have laid Him, and I will take Him away."

Was it her tears that blinded Mary's eyes that morning? Was it the grief of her heart that made all the world seem to move in slow motion—unreal and phantomlike? It all changed when He said one word. He called her name: "Mary."

"My sheep hear My voice, and I know them, and they follow Me" (John 10:27). Although she had not recognized Him before, at the sound of her name, Mary's heart pounded, her breath caught, and she moved the hair from her face and stared in awe, in terror, in joy rising like a flood.

"Rabboni!" she cried. "My teacher!" And she lunged for Jesus and held His feet. Beyond hope, beyond her wildest dreams, He stood there. Not a ghost. Not a spirit. Not an illusion or some wishful thinking. Her Jesus—flesh and blood, the wounds still visible, but transfigured, shining in glory. Her Jesus.

And the tears came again, but this time of another sort. These were not the sobs of despair, but the tears that brim from a cup that runs over with joy. It was a tender moment, but the joys were only beginning. Jesus had work for Mary to do, an embassy for her to carry out. He sent her first to His apostles to give them the message that He lives and that He is preparing to ascend to His Father and their Father, to His God and their God. Death was not the end of Him, and so it will not be the end of Mary or of the disciples.

Nor will death be the end of you. Jesus has changed forever how we live, how we grieve, and how we die. Oh, we still feel in our bones how wrong death is, how unnatural, and we hate it with a passion. But Jesus has made it something we never have to fear—not ever again. For by His death and resurrection, Jesus has wounded death itself, dealt it a mortal blow from which it will never recover. He came out of its stinking gullet alive again, never to die again, and His promise to Mary, to His apostles, and to all His baptized children is that He will bring each and every one of us through the hole He punched in death into the home He has prepared for us with His Father.

To strengthen your faith in His resurrection victory, Jesus continues to put into your dying bodies His body that was on the tree, atoning for all your sin; that was in the tomb, sanctifying your grave; and that Mary held in the garden that first Easter Day. He pours down your throat the blood that He shed to wipe out the sin of the world, and He reminds you that it is all for you. He whispers to each of you, "As death could not hold Me, so it will not hold you, My child. Baptized into My undying life, I will bring you out of death just as I came out of it—alive, never to die again. And then the celebration will really begin!"

Alleluia! Alleuia! Christ is risen!

He is risen indeed! Alleluia!

CHILDREN'S MESSAGES

Ash Wednesday

WHAT MAKES JESUS SAD?

MESSAGE

Hello! Today I brought some sad faces to help us play a game. *Give one sad face to each of five (or more) children.* Every time I say something that would make Jesus sad, I want you to hold up your card. Ready? *Read the following statements, allow the children to hold up their cards. Discuss why Jesus would be sad.*

VISUAL

• Five or more sad faces on 5 × 5-inch heavy paper squares

• One happy face on a 5 × 5-inch heavy paper square

READ

Joel 2:12–19

SUMMARY

The Lord forgives us when we are truly sorry for our sins.

• You leave your brother's bicycle outside, and it gets rained on.

• You talk back to your mom.

• You hit your little brother.

• Your mom tells you to clean your room, but you do not do it.

• You do not like the girl next door.

Wow! You held up your sad faces all the time. Because we are not perfect, we often do and think bad things. That makes Jesus sad. It makes us sad too. We want to be good, and we try very hard, but we often do things that make Jesus unhappy. When you have done something wrong, how do you show that you are sorry? *Accept answers such as cry, apologize, try to do better, etc.*

Many years ago, God's people had the same problem we do. They did many things that made God unhappy. God told them to be sorry for what they had done. He told them to cry and ask for forgiveness. Then He forgave them.

God also wants us to be sorry when we do bad things. He knows if we are really sad that we hurt Him. Best of all, God sent Jesus to be our Savior. Jesus died on the cross to forgive every bad thought, every bad word, and every bad thing we do. He loves us and helps us do better.

And when we do something wrong, He waits for us to come to Him and say we are sorry. Because Jesus died for us, our sad faces turn into this. ***Hold up happy face.*** We know Jesus forgives us and cares for us, and that puts a smile on our faces!

Let us close with a little prayer. Thank You, Jesus . . . for dying for my sins . . . and forgiving me when I sin. . . . Help me do things . . . that make You happy. . . . Amen.

Midweek 2

BETRAYED!

MESSAGE

Today I have a bag containing a wonderful invention. This invention can do all kinds of things, and you should not be without it. It can make something beautiful, and it can even do math. Only one of you can get this gift, so raise your hand if you want it. ***Choose someone to open the bag and take out the pencil.***

Some of you do not seem to think my gift was very good. A pencil can make beautiful things when you draw pictures, and it can help you with math when you write numbers. I told you the truth. I just made it sound better than it was, and you were disappointed. I am your friend, so you thought my gift would be something special, and you do not think it was. When all I gave you was a pencil, you felt like I had played a trick on you.

Do you know there is a word that tells how you feel when a friend does not act like a friend? ***Hold up the poster board so the children and congregation can see the word.*** The word is *betrayed*.

Jesus was betrayed by a man who pretended to be His friend. Judas was one of Jesus' disciples. He listened to Jesus teach. He ate with Jesus, and he walked with Jesus. But Judas decided to give Jesus to the people who wanted to kill Him. Those people promised Judas money if he would show them where Jesus was. Jesus could see inside Judas's heart, and Jesus knew the wicked plans Judas was making. How it hurt Jesus to know that His friend would betray Him!

But before we wonder how Judas could do such a horrible thing, I must ask you something: do you know that every time we tell a lie or do something bad we betray Jesus too? We have told Jesus we are

VISUAL

• A pencil inside a closed paper bag

• Sheet of poster board with word *betrayed* written on it

READ

Matthew 26:20–25

SUMMARY

Like Judas, we betray Jesus, but Jesus still loves and forgives us.

His friends, but then we do things that hurt Him. How sad that makes Jesus!

Jesus came to earth to help us. He died on the cross to wash away all those bad things we do. He sends the Holy Spirit to help us live as His friends. We do not want to betray Jesus, and we thank Him every day for taking away our sins.

Pray with the children for God's strength to help them live for Him.

Midweek 3

BEING A FRIEND

MESSAGE

Sometimes it is hard to get up on Sunday morning, so I am sure you will not have any trouble remembering this sentence: "I am too tired." *Have the children repeat the sentence.* I need some help today. Whenever I say the word *please*, I want you to say, "I am too tired."

I brought along this knotted sock. *Show sock.* Maybe you can help me undo it. Please? *Wait for the children to respond with "I am too tired."*

It is too bad you cannot help me. But, look, maybe this is something you can do. *Show puzzle.* I brought this puzzle, and it would go together faster if I had help. Please? *Wait for response.* I guess the puzzle will not get done.

VISUAL

- Knotted sock
- Puzzle
- Cell phone

READ

Matthew 26:36–45

SUMMARY

Jesus died to forgive us when our apathy hurts others.

Now here is something you might like to do. There is an older lady who needs some friends. She is lonely and sad, and I know a visit from you would cheer her up. *Show cell phone.* I have the phone right here, so I can call her and tell her you will come. Please? *Wait for response.*

When we will not do something because we are tired or do not feel like doing it or simply do not care, it is called "apathy." *Have the children say the word.* When you said, "I am too tired," you were showing apathy. Let me ask you a question. Which of these jobs was most important? *Summarize jobs, holding up each object. Affirm response that visiting was most important.*

Apathy can hurt other people. When Jesus went into the Garden of Gethsemane to pray the night before He died, He asked the disciples to wait with Him. Jesus knew He was going to die, and He wanted His friends to be there for Him. But do you know what the disciples did? They fell asleep! Jesus had to pray all by Himself on the hardest night of His whole life.

Sometimes we are like those disciples. We do not want to help a friend or do a job our parents ask us to do. We are full of apathy. The good news is that Jesus forgave His disciples, and He forgives us too. Jesus died for the sin of apathy, and He helps us to be better friends to others.

Pray with me. Jesus, please forgive me . . . when I do not help others. . . . Take away my apathy . . . and help me live for You. . . . Amen.

Midweek 4

I Do Not Know the Man

Message

I want to play a game with you. I am going to lay down a sheet of paper and turn around. ***Choose one child.*** I want you to point to someone. That person will pick up the sheet of paper, tear it in half, and lay both pieces of paper on the floor. I'll close my eyes so I don't see who tears the paper. ***Allow time for the action, then turn around.***

Visual

• A blank sheet of paper

• A sheet of paper or poster board with the words "I do not know the man" in large print

• A Bible

Read

Matthew 26:69–75

Summary

Jesus forgives our sins of denial just as He forgave Peter.

I don't want you to tell me who tore the paper. I will ask each of you if you did it, and I want you to say "no," even if you're the one who tore the paper. ***Ask each child.*** You all denied tearing the paper, but one of you is lying. Now, I want you to raise your hand if you tore the paper. ***Wait for child to raise hand.*** At first you denied tearing the paper, but now you are telling the truth.

Denial means "lying." I have another sheet of paper with words written on it. We can read the sentence together. It says, "I do not know the man." Jesus' friend Peter lied when he said those words. He was outside the room where the leaders took Jesus after His arrest. People standing with Peter said, "You are one of Jesus' friends." Peter was afraid he might be arrested, so he said: ***Let the children read the sentence aloud.*** Suddenly, Peter remembered that Jesus said he would deny Him. Peter felt so badly about his lies that he went outside and cried.

There are times when we deny Jesus too. When we do not listen to our parents, we are acting as though we do not know Jesus. When we lie or are mean to others, we are denying that Jesus is our friend. We are saying: ***Let the children read the sentence aloud.***

Jesus saw that Peter was sorry, and He forgave Peter. Jesus sees the bad things we do, too, but He also sees when we are sorry and need for-

46

giveness. Let me read what God tells us in the Bible. ***Read 1 John 1:9a.*** "Confess" means to be sorry. Even when we deny Jesus is our friend by the wrong things we do, He still loves us and forgives us. What a wonderful God we have!

Close with a prayer that thanks Jesus for His forgiveness.

Midweek 5

NOT WHAT IT SEEMS

MESSAGE

Pretend that you've never seen any of the things I'm going to show you. Pretend that you do not know what these items do.

Look at this odd-looking contraption. **Show unopened umbrella.** This will keep you dry on a rainy day. Does it look like it can keep you dry? **Wait for negative answer.** Let me show you something wonderful. **Open umbrella.** Presto! Now it will keep you dry!

Here is another great invention. This little gadget helps hold papers together. Does it look like it can do that? **Wait for negative answer.** Let me show you how it works. **Staple papers.** What a surprise!

If you had never seen these things before, I think you would be surprised at what they can do. The umbrella keeps us dry, and the stapler does hold papers together, though they don't look like they can do those things.

When Jesus was a prisoner, He told Pilate, the governor, that He was a king. Then soldiers mocked Jesus for saying this. *Mocking* means to make fun of someone you think is lying. The soldiers beat Jesus, they dressed Him in a purple robe and put a crown of thorns on His head. They said, "Hail, King of the Jews!" Those soldiers were mocking Jesus because He did not look like a king. He did not have a crown or live in a castle. But we know Jesus is the greatest King who ever lived, and He rules heaven and earth. Jesus was telling the truth when He said He was a king.

The beatings and the thorns hurt Jesus, but what hurt most was that people did not believe He was a king. Jesus wants us to know He is a king who will someday take us to His kingdom—heaven. He wants us to know He's a good king who loves and cares for us. Most of all, Jesus

VISUAL

- Umbrella
- Stapler
- Sheets of paper

READ

Matthew 27:27–31

SUMMARY

Although Jesus did not appear to be a king, He is King of heaven and earth.

wants us to know that He suffered and died to take the punishment for the bad things we do. He really is our Savior King.

Pray, thanking Jesus for leaving heaven and coming to earth to save us. Praise Him for being King over heaven and earth.

Midweek 6

ALL ALONE

MESSAGE

Lay poster board word-side down in front of you. I have a new word for you to learn. But before I show it to you, I want you to make a promise. I want you to promise that no matter what happens up here, you will stay right where you are and be very quiet. Will you do that? ***Wait for affirmation.*** Good! ***Hold up word.*** The word I have for you to learn is *abandoned*. Wait just a minute. . . . ***Get up and leave. Stay away long enough for the children to be uncomfortable, but not so long that they become restless.***

VISUAL

- Poster board with word *abandoned* written on it
- Marking pen
- Bible

READ

Matthew 27:45–48

SUMMARY

God the Father temporarily abandoned Jesus because our Savior carried our sins to the cross.

I am back! Thank you for keeping your promise. It was a surprise when I left you alone, wasn't it? How did you feel? ***Accept responses such as "scared," "worried," "alone."*** Another word telling how you felt is the word *abandoned*. ***Hold up poster board so the children and the congregation can see the word.*** It did not feel good when I left you alone, but what if everyone in the church walked out and you were sitting here all by yourself? How would you feel then? ***Wait for responses.*** Yes, being alone, being abandoned, can be a pretty scary thing.

There is another word that means "abandoned," and I am going to write it on this poster board. ***Write the word "forsaken" on the poster board.*** Let me read from the Bible what Jesus said on the cross. ***Read Matthew 27:46b.*** Who had forsaken or abandoned Jesus? ***Accept responses such as "God" or "His Father."*** How do you think Jesus felt? ***Accept responses such as "scared," "worried," "alone," "sad."***

God abandoned Jesus on the cross because Jesus was taking all our sins on Himself. We cannot see sins, the bad things we do, but they are very real. God the Father hates sin so much that for a little while He

50

could not stay with Jesus because there was so much sin with Him. Even the sky grew dark and ugly when Jesus was on the cross.

Jesus loved us so much that He took the punishment for our sins by giving up His life. Oh, we still do bad things, but we know God forgives us because Jesus did the hard work of saving us. Now we look clean to God the Father, not dirty with sin. We can thank Jesus for dying for us, though it meant God abandoned Him because of all our sins.

Pray, thanking God for His salvation.

Maundy Thursday

Soul Food

MESSAGE

Today I brought something you have seen before. ***Show menu.*** Yes, it is a menu. A menu lists the different foods a restaurant serves. We usually eat three meals a day. Sometimes we might go out to eat. Why is eating so important? ***Accept answers such as "need food to live," "keeps us healthy," "keeps us strong," etc.***

I am going to show you another menu. ***Show handmade menu.*** This one says "Soul Food" on the front. The food in this menu is not meant for our bodies. The food in this menu is meant for our souls. We cannot see our souls, but that is the part of us that loves God and cares about godly things. ***Open menu and read menu items.***

If we ate one little piece of bread and drank one little sip of wine, would it be a good lunch? ***Wait for negative answer.*** No, this is not enough healthy food for our bodies. The bread and wine are there to help us get the food that is important for our souls. Our menu says: "bread AND body" and "wine AND blood." The body and blood part are the food that is meant for our souls. We cannot see Jesus' body, and we cannot see His blood, but Jesus tells us that they are right there in the bread and wine. And they are *free*! Jesus gave His body and blood for our souls, and it did not cost us anything. He gave up His life because He loves us.

We need food for our body to stay alive and healthy. Soul food does the same thing for our souls. We call this little meal "the Lord's Supper." Every time a person goes to the Lord's Supper, Jesus gives the special food of His body and His blood to forgive the bad things we do. The

---

VISUAL

• Restaurant menu (many restaurants have menus on the Internet)

• Handmade menu with "Soul Food" on the front. Inside list "bread and body" and "wine and blood." Across from these listings, write "FREE."

READ

Exodus 24:3–11

SUMMARY

The Lord's Supper assures us of God's forgiveness and strengthens our faith.

Lord's Supper makes faith strong, showing us how much God loves us and is always with us.

We eat food to keep our bodies healthy. Jesus gives us soul food to keep our souls healthy. We can thank God for giving us such wonderful food for our souls.

Close with prayer, thanking God for the gift of the Sacrament.

Good Friday

FIXING SIN

MESSAGE

Today I brought a few things that need fixing. ***Open first bag and lay out items.*** This paper is torn, this sheet of paper needs some writing removed, and this button needs to be sewed on a shirt.

I brought along another bag too. ***Open second bag and lay out items.*** Who can tell me which of these I would use to fix the torn paper? ***Allow the children to respond.*** That is right, I would use the tape.

VISUAL

• Bag with torn paper, paper with writing in pencil, button

• Bag with clear tape, eraser, spool of thread with needle in it

READ

Isaiah 53:1–6

SUMMARY

Jesus suffered and died to bring us healing for our sins.

Now, who can tell me that I would use to remove the writing from this sheet of paper? ***Allow the children to respond.*** That is right, I would use the eraser.

Finally, who can tell me what I would use to sew a button on a shirt? ***Allow the children to respond.*** Yes, I would need a needle and thread. Finding the right things to make the repairs was pretty easy.

There is something in our lives that needs fixing, and finding the answer is not as easy as what we just did. Our sins need fixing more than anything else. What are sins? ***Accept answers such as "bad things we do," "things God says not to do," etc.***

Adam and Eve were the first ones to sin when they ate the fruit that God said not to eat. After that, everyone who has been born has sin in them. That means you and I have sin too. We cannot erase our sins or wash them away. We cannot see them, but sin is with us every day.

God sees us, and He sees our sin. He knew there was only one way to fix it. He made a plan that His Son, who had no sin at all, would have to come to earth. He would have to die to take the punishment for our sins on Him. Then we would be clean before God.

So Jesus came to earth. He was born, lived a perfect life, and died on the cross. Before He died, Jesus was beaten and hurt. Terrible things happened to Jesus, but He loved us so much that He let these bad things happen. It was the only way He could take away our sins.

We still sin, but Jesus fixed it when He suffered and died. If Jesus had not died for us, we could never go to heaven. Our sins would keep us out. Now God forgives our sins because of what Jesus did, and someday we will be with Him in heaven.

Pray with children, thanking Jesus for taking away our sin.

Easter Sunday
DARK AND LIGHT

MESSAGE

This morning I am going to pass out circles so some of you can help me. *Give double-sided circles to older children.* I am going to say some words, and I want you to hold up the black side of the circle if the word reminds you of darkness. If the word reminds you of light, hold up the white side. Ready? *Say the following words, and wait for appropriate responses: sunshine, a cave, midnight, a swimming pool, the moon, a closet.* Great job!

VISUAL

• Five or more circles, 4–5 inches in diameter, black on one side, white on the other

• Circle that is half black and half white

READ

John 20:11–16

SUMMARY

The blackness of death and sin was overcome when Jesus rose from the dead.

Now it will get harder. The black circle means something bad, and the white circle means something good. Ready? *Say the following words, and lead to correct responses if necessary: sin, the devil, God, death, heaven.*

I have just one more phrase for you: Jesus on the cross. *Allow children to show circles. Some may show the dark circle, some light.*

"Jesus on the cross" was harder, because on the cross, sin and death, which remind us of darkness, met Jesus, who reminds us of light. *Hold up half-black, half-white circle.* When Jesus died on the cross, the punishment for all the sins of the world went with Him. The devil was there, too, and he was happy when Jesus died. That is the dark part. The devil thought he had won. He thought everyone in the world belonged to him now. He thought he was rid of Jesus.

But three days later, Jesus surprised everyone, including the devil. What was that surprise? Yes, Jesus rose from the dead! Jesus was stronger than the devil, stronger than all our sins, and stronger than death. The light of Jesus, who was God and man, was stronger than the blackness of sin and death.

Jesus loved us so much that He died on a cross so we would not have to be afraid of the devil or sin or death anymore. Now our lives are bright because Jesus saved us. Because Jesus rose from the dead, we will live again after we die. We belong to Jesus, and someday we will live with Him in heaven, a place of beauty and light.

Pray, thanking Jesus for being the light of the world.

BIBLE
STUDIES

<u>STUDENT</u>

Ash Wednesday

A WOUNDED SAVIOR FOR A WOUNDED PEOPLE

THEME VERSE

But He was wounded for our transgressions; He was crushed for our iniquities; upon Him was the chastisement that brought us peace, and with His stripes we are healed. (Isaiah 53:5)

TEXT

Joel 2:12–19

INTRODUCTION

The Old Testament reading for Ash Wednesday may appear stern to us, but it sounds a summons that we need to hear. Joel works like a skillful surgeon who must cut with a scalpel in order to heal us from the wounds of sin and death. The prophet calls us to acknowledge that we are indeed wounded by sin and death, because such humble confession also receives the wounded Savior, who brings eternal healing.

BIBLE STUDY

1. Skim over Joel 1:1–2:11. The prophet gives a stark, somber picture of God's judgment as he calls God's people to repent. Read Jeremiah 3:6–11 and Isaiah 1:2–6. What leads God to threaten His own people with judgment?

2. The Augsburg Confession refers to original sin as "a disease and original vice" (AC II 2) that actually separates us from our merciful God. According to Matthew 9:12, how does our Lord Jesus teach us to view our sinful state? According to Romans 5:12 and Hebrews 2:14–15, what else accompanies sin and thus wounds us?

3. As we begin the season of Lent, Joel calls us to return to the Lord God with all our heart, "with fasting, with weeping, and with mourning" (2:12). How do such practices facilitate our returning to the Lord?

4. According to Matthew 6:1–18, especially verses 1, 2, 5, and 16, how does our Lord Jesus teach us to practice acts of piety such as fasting, weeping, and mourning?

5. What does Joel mean by "rend your hearts and not your garments" (2:13)? See Psalm 32:5; 51:1–5, 17; Philippians 3:3; and Colossians 2:11–12.

6. How does our Lord Jesus Christ reveal that our God "is gracious and merciful, slow to anger, and abounding in steadfast love" (Joel 2:13)? See Matthew 4:1–4; John 11:35; and Luke 19:41–42.

7. How does our Lord Jesus heal us from our sickness of sin and death, along with the wounds they bring into our lives? See Isaiah 53:4–6; 2 Corinthians 5:21; and 1 Peter 2:24–25.

8. The prophet calls us to practice much more than a private, individualistic form of repentance and returning to the Lord. According to Joel 2:15–17, where does the returning, fasting, weeping, and mourning find its fuller expression?

9. According to Joel 2:16, to whom does the time of returning to the Lord apply? According to Joel 2:17, how do the clergy participate in the time of repenting?

10. How does the season of Lent draw us out of our privatized, individualized lives so that we can return to the Lord in the assembly of His congregation? See also Hebrews 10:19–25 and Colossians 3:12–17.

11. Our text ends with God's promise of restoration in Joel 2:18–19. How does such a promise motivate us and sustain us in our time of repentance and returning to the Lord?

CONCLUSION

Joel exhorts us to return to the Lord with all our hearts, with fasting, with weeping, with mourning, and by rending our hearts. It may feel quite uncomfortable, but God's mercy makes such healing regimens salutary. Joel calls us to return to God, "for He is gracious and merciful, slow to anger, and abounding in steadfast love" (2:13). We begin our Lenten journey by confessing that we are fatally wounded by sin and death, but we also rejoice that God mercifully sends a wounded Savior to heal us wounded people.

LEADER

Ash Wednesday

A WOUNDED SAVIOR FOR A WOUNDED PEOPLE

THEME VERSE

But He was wounded for our transgressions; He was crushed for our iniquities; upon Him was the chastisement that brought us peace, and with His stripes we are healed. (Isaiah 53:5)

TEXT

Joel 2:12–19

INTRODUCTION

The Old Testament reading for Ash Wednesday may appear stern to us, but it sounds a summons that we need to hear. Joel works like a skillful surgeon who must cut with a scalpel in order to heal us from the wounds of sin and death. The prophet calls us to acknowledge that we are indeed wounded by sin and death, because such humble confession also receives the wounded Savior, who brings eternal healing.

BIBLE STUDY ANSWERS AND COMMENTARY

1. God threatens to judge His people because they first forsake Him. Jeremiah 3:6–11 compares God's faithless people to adulterous women who worship anyone or anything other than God. Isaiah 1:2–6 compares God's people to children who rebel and deal corruptly. When God's people "have forsaken the Lord" and "have despised the Holy One of Israel" (Isaiah 1:4), they risk bringing God's judgment upon themselves. Isaiah also compares this sinful rebellion to a disease in which "the whole head is sick, and the whole heart faint" (1:5).

2. Jesus says, "Those who are well have no need of a physician, but those who are sick" (Matthew 9:12). Our Lord comes to heal us from our congenital birth defect of sin. The plague of death accompanies our disease of sin. "Death spread to all men because all sinned" (Romans 5:12). Our Lord comes to "destroy the one who has the power of death, that is, the devil, and deliver all those who through fear of death were subject to lifelong slavery" (Hebrews 2:14–15).

3. During Lent, we ponder how sin and death wound us: we do not love God or our neighbors as we should. When Joel calls us to "return to the Lord [our] God" (2:13), he exhorts us to do this with our whole heart, with fasting that denies our selfish desires, and with weeping and mourning over our sins. Such activities do not earn God's forgiveness. Rather, they work like a defibrillator that stops the heart from beating irregularly so it may again beat properly. Repenting with the whole heart, with fasting, and with weeping and mourning stops us from loving ourselves so that we can, by God's grace, love God and our neighbors.

4. Jesus teaches us to do our acts of piety in humility before God and not to be seen by others. He certainly approves of giving alms, praying, and fasting, and He gives the proper way to practice such acts of piety— in humility toward God and not for public show. When we give alms, pray, and fast, we focus on the God "who sees in secret" (Matthew 6:4). Jesus says, "Your Father who sees in secret will reward you" (6:4), that is, He gives us His grace and mercy in Christ Jesus. In our acts of piety, we deny ourselves and focus on the God who saves and heals us through His Son.

5. Rending our hearts and not our garments means acknowledging and confessing our sins to God and receiving His forgiveness (Psalm 32:5). "The sacrifices of God are a broken spirit," and God will not despise "a broken and contrite heart" (Psalm 51:17). We can rend our hearts because we "put no confidence in the flesh" (Philippians 3:3). Instead, we put all confidence in Jesus Christ and His healing of forgiveness. We can put "off the body of the flesh" because we have "been buried with [Christ] in baptism, in which [we] were also raised with Him through faith in the powerful working of God, who raised Him from the dead" (Colossians 2:11–12). Lent teaches us to live in our Baptism!

6. Our Lord Jesus showed His great compassion and mercy by doing the very things that Joel exhorts God's people to do. Jesus fasted and did not serve Himself (Matthew 4:1–4). He wept at the death of Lazarus (John 11:35) and showed that He came to heal us from death. He also wept over unbelieving Jerusalem (Luke 19:41–42) and showed that God grieves when His people turn from Him. Our Lord fasts, weeps, and mourns over how sin and death have wounded us, and He enables us to fast, weep, and mourn as we receive His healing mercy and forgiveness.

7. Our Lord Jesus heals us from sin and death with forgiveness that flows from His wounds on the cross. Our Lord "was wounded for our transgressions . . . and with His stripes we are healed" (Isaiah 53:5). Our iniquity causes us to live self-centeredly, but "the Lord has laid on Him the iniquity of us all" (Isaiah 53:6). Our Lord takes our wounds of sin and death upon Himself, because God "made Him to be sin who knew no sin, so that in Him we might become the righteousness of God" (2 Corinthians 5:21). Jesus "bore our sins in His body on the tree, that we might die to sin and live to righteousness" (1 Peter 2:24). As we live in Jesus' forgiveness, the wounds of our self-centeredness begin to heal.

8. Our repentance and returning to God are not solo activities. They take place in the Christian congregation, the "solemn assembly" (Joel 2:15). Our Lenten returning to the Lord, fasting, weeping, and mourning also take place in the congregation. We do not perform such acts of devotion for the praise of men, but we do join our fellow Christians in such acts of repentant, faithful devotion. Because we all need healing from the same wounds of sin and death, we can encourage one another along the way.

9. Returning to the Lord, repenting, fasting, mourning, and weeping apply to everyone. All people need to return to the Lord in repentance. Elders (mature Christians) need to repent, fast, weep, and mourn, just as much as children and "even nursing infants" (Joel 2:16). The bridegroom and the bride also set aside their joyous wedding plans in order to take part in the congregational repentance and returning to the Lord. Every human being needs to be healed from sin and death. In verse 17, the clergy lead the weeping as they prayerfully cry out for God to spare His people.

10. When our wounded Savior heals us from our disease of sin and death, He liberates us from focusing on ourselves. We are restored to life with God and with our neighbors, especially in the family of the Church. Hebrews 10 speaks of Christ's blood making us clean, and then exhorts us to stir up one another to good works, especially as we meet together in worship. Colossians 3:12–17 exhorts us to live not in the privacy of our own devotion, but in the community of Christ's Holy Church, loving and edifying one another in Christ's healing forgiveness. During Lent, we leave behind our self-centered ways that wound us, and we cling to Christ and our fellow Christians.

11. Our Lord Jesus, wounded for our iniquity, shows that our gracious God has "had pity on His people" (Joel 2:18). The time of fasting, weeping, and mourning over our sin and death will give way to the joyous, satisfying prosperity of God's mercy and healing in eternity. During Lent, we fast, weep, and mourn over our sin, but during Easter we receive a foretaste of the feast to come in God's perfect healing and life!

Conclusion

Joel exhorts us to return to the Lord with all our hearts, with fasting, with weeping, with mourning, and by rending our hearts. It may feel quite uncomfortable, but God's mercy makes such healing regimens salutary. Joel calls us to return to God, "for He is gracious and merciful, slow to anger, and abounding in steadfast love" (2:13). We begin our Lenten journey by confessing that we are fatally wounded by sin and death, but we also rejoice that God mercifully sends a wounded Savior to heal us wounded people.

STUDENT

Midweek 2

THE WOUND OF BETRAYAL

THEME VERSE

"For the Son of Man goes as it has been determined, but woe to that man by whom He is betrayed!" (Luke 22:22)

TEXT

Matthew 26:20–25

INTRODUCTION

During Lent, we focus on our Lord Jesus Christ, who became wounded with our sin and death in order to heal us from those very wounds. In this lesson, we concentrate on a most painful wound: betrayal. No strong bravado can overcome the wound of betrayal. However, when our Lord Jesus Christ suffers the wound of our betrayal, He heals us and restores us to faith in our heavenly Father.

BIBLE STUDY

1. Read Genesis 37:12–14, 18–28; and 2 Samuel 15:1–4, 13–17. Note the wounds of betrayal experienced by two of God's people. What leads the betrayers in each story to inflict these wounds? How does the betrayed person in each story suffer from the betrayal?

2. Read Matthew 26:14–16 to see how Judas planned to betray Jesus. What is significant about the thirty pieces of silver? See Exodus 21:32.

3. In what setting must Jesus endure the wound of betrayal? See

65

Matthew 26:17–19 and 26:26–29. How does this setting make that wound even more painful?

4. When Jesus says, "Truly, I say to you, one of you will betray Me" (Matthew 26:21), what message does He send to the betrayer? What message does He send to the other disciples?

5. According to Matthew 26:22, how do the disciples react to Jesus' announcement about His coming betrayal? What salutary lesson can we learn from this reaction?

6. How does Jesus reveal who will betray Him? See Matthew 26:23. In Matthew 26:25, how does Jesus answer Judas's question, "Is it I, Rabbi?"

7. Read John 13:21–30 for more details on how Jesus reveals His betrayer. How do Peter and John prompt Jesus to expose His betrayer (verses 23–25)? In John's account, what happened to Judas after Jesus dipped the bread? What is the significance of John's comment in verse 30, "And it was night"?

8. What does Jesus mean in Matthew 26:24 when He says, "The Son of Man goes as it is written of Him, but woe to that man by whom the Son of Man is betrayed"? If Jesus is destined to suffer and die, why must He be betrayed?

9. Read Matthew 26:47–50. How does Judas finally betray Jesus? How does his kiss (verse 49) make the betrayal even more bitter?

10. Matthew 27:3–10 tells us how Judas "changed his mind and brought back the thirty pieces of silver to the chief priests and the elders" (27:3). Verses 9–10 quote from Zechariah 11:12–13. What message did the prophet Zechariah give when he threw his thirty pieces of silver "into the house of the Lord, to the potter" (Zechariah 11:13)?

11. Why is it necessary for our Lord Jesus to suffer the wound of betrayal at the hands of Judas, one of His chosen twelve disciples?

12. How might we risk betraying our Lord Jesus? Hint: Remember the context in which Jesus' betrayal takes place, Matthew 26:26–28. Also see 1 Corinthians 11:27. According to 2 Timothy 2:11–13, what comfort and hope do we have? How does Jesus' faithfulness in the face of betrayal give us His grace and mercy? See Hebrews 4:14–16.

Conclusion

When our Lord Jesus suffers betrayal from Judas, He suffers the wounds that our sin and death have inflicted on us. Our human selfishness leads us to betray those closest to us, but our Lord's patient suffering and enduring love show us the way of His healing for our betrayal of Him. The Meal that Jesus instituted as He was betrayed gives us forgiveness for our betrayal of Him and strengthens us to remain faithful.

Leader

Midweek 2

The Wound of Betrayal

Theme Verse

"For the Son of Man goes as it has been determined, but woe to that man by whom He is betrayed!" (Luke 22:22)

Text

Matthew 26:20–25

Introduction

During Lent, we focus on our Lord Jesus Christ, who became wounded with our sin and death in order to heal us from those very wounds. In this lesson, we concentrate on a most painful wound: betrayal. No strong bravado can overcome the wound of betrayal. However, when our Lord Jesus Christ suffers the wound of our betrayal, He heals us and restores us to faith in our heavenly Father.

BIBLE STUDY ANSWERS AND COMMENTARY

1. In Genesis 37, Joseph suffers betrayal from his brothers. At first, the brothers want to kill Joseph because of his dreams (37:18; see 37:1–11), but then they settle on betraying Joseph by selling him to Midianite traders (37:25–28). For years, Joseph suffered separation from his family, slavery, and imprisonment. In 2 Samuel 15:1–4, David suffers betrayal from his son Absalom, as Absalom tries to wrest the kingdom and the loyalty of the people away from David. According to 2 Samuel 15:13–17, David suffers the shame of fleeing for his life and leaving Jerusalem.

2. When Judas arranged to betray Jesus, he agreed to receive thirty pieces of silver, the ancient price for a slave who had been gored by an ox (see Exodus 21:32). In Judas's mind, the Lord Jesus was worth little more than a slave.

3. Jesus endures the wound of betrayal as He celebrates the Passover with His disciples. From this meal, He would institute the Lord's Supper, the Christian fulfillment of the ancient Passover. This makes Jesus' wound of betrayal that much more painful, because sharing a meal together meant close friendship among those around the table, but Judas used this occasion to betray Jesus. Although the Lord's Supper focuses on Jesus' forgiveness of sins, Judas would commit the sin of betrayal against Him.

4. When Jesus says, "One of you will betray Me," He sends a message to all of His disciples at once. To Judas, Jesus' words uncover his plan of betrayal while still protecting his reputation. They also give Judas the opportunity to confess his plot and thus be saved. For the other disciples, Jesus' words invite them to examine themselves, because any of them could also fall to the temptation to betray and forsake Jesus.

5. As a result of Jesus' pronouncement that one would betray Him, each of the disciples shares in the sorrow and examines himself, asking, "Is it I, Lord?" Every Christian can learn a salutary lesson from this. First, it is possible for Christians to turn away from and betray their Lord when they rely on their own strength and reason in understanding and trusting how their Lord Jesus works for them. Second, self-examination is quite healthy for Jesus' followers, especially because it leads them to rely not on themselves, but on their faithful Savior.

6. In Matthew 26:23, Jesus reveals His betrayer by saying, "He who has dipped his hand in the dish with Me will betray Me." That is, the betrayer would be a close friend of Jesus. Here Jesus makes another attempt to turn Judas from his betrayal and openly confess his sin. But Judas does not do so. Instead, he asks the same self-evaluating question that the others had asked: "Is it I, Rabbi?" (26:25). Jesus responds: "You have said so," that is, "Your own words give you away."

7. The Gospel of John gives more details about how Jesus reveals His betrayer. After He mentions that one of them will betray Him, Simon Peter asks John, who is sitting next to Jesus, to ask who it is (John 13:23–25). Whereas Matthew's account makes a general statement about the betrayer dipping bread with Jesus, John's account specifies that Jesus dipped the bread and handed it to Judas to indicate the specific disciple who would betray Him. After Judas took the bread from Jesus' hand, John 13:27 says, "Satan entered into him." Knowing that He must be betrayed in order to suffer all that we suffer, Jesus said, "What you are going to do, do quickly." When John 13:30 says, "And it was night," it may have a meaning less literal than the time of day. While these events certainly happened at night, the "night" of verse 30 could also be seen as a comment on the darkness of Judas's soul and his act of betrayal.

8. While Jesus must certainly be betrayed and handed over to sinful men in order to suffer, die, and rise again for the life of the world, His betrayer is also responsible for his sin of betrayal. God's eternal plan for saving the world does not cancel out Judas's responsibility in betraying Jesus. Still, Jesus must be betrayed in order that He may be our faithful High Priest who is able to sympathize with our weaknesses and be tempted as we are in every respect, except without sin (see Hebrews 4:15). Thus Jesus enters the very depth and breadth of our sin and wickedness in order to rescue us from our sin and death.

9. Judas betrays Jesus by leading a band of soldiers to arrest Him. He identifies Jesus with a kiss. Because a kiss shows utmost friendship and intimacy, Judas's kiss only adds to the bitterness of Jesus' wound of betrayal. One who should be a close friend and display the affection of a friend now turns from Jesus and hands Him over to be mockingly tried, falsely convicted, and cruelly tortured and executed. Bitter betrayal indeed!

10. Zechariah's words refer to a shepherd, God, who did not shepherd His wayward sheep because they first rejected Him. Zechariah threw the wages of thirty pieces of silver into the temple as a sign of the separation between God and His people. We see the same things happening in the betrayal and crucifixion of our Lord. The people of Israel (the sheep) actually reject their divine Shepherd (Jesus), and thirty pieces of silver again ring in the temple as an indicator that the Son of God is being cut off from His people.

11. Betrayal hurts most when it comes from one who is very close. Thus Jesus suffers the wound of betrayal at the hands of one of His closest disciples, Judas Iscariot. In this way, our Lord identifies with us when we are betrayed by a close friend or loved one, as well as when we actually inflict the wound of betrayal on someone close to us. Jesus absorbs into Himself our wounds of betrayal, with all of their bitterness and pain, as He takes our sins upon Himself to forgive and heal us.

12. We run the risk of betraying our Lord Jesus by not recognizing His body and His blood—both His real presence in the Sacrament and in His Body, the Church—at the Lord's Supper. See 1 Corinthians 11:27. However, our comfort comes from this: "if we are faithless, He remains faithful—for He cannot deny Himself" (2 Timothy 2:13). Because Jesus has suffered our wound of betrayal, we can "draw near to the throne of grace, that we may receive mercy and find grace to help in time of need" (Hebrews 4:16).

Conclusion

When our Lord Jesus suffers betrayal from Judas, He suffers the wounds that our sin and death have inflicted on us. Our human selfishness leads us to betray those closest to us, but our Lord's patient suffering and enduring love show us the way of His healing for our betrayal of Him. The Meal that Jesus instituted as He was betrayed gives us forgiveness for our betrayal of Him and strengthens us to remain faithful.

Midweek 3

THE WOUND OF APATHY

THEME VERSE

And [Jesus] said to Peter, "So, could you not watch with Me one hour? Watch and pray that you may not enter into temptation. The spirit indeed is willing, but the flesh is weak." (Matthew 26:40–41)

TEXT

Matthew 26:36–45

INTRODUCTION

When Jesus suffers the weight of the world's sin, He also suffers the wound of our apathy. The word *apathy* means "without feeling or concern." When the disciples fall asleep during Jesus' hour of intense suffering, they show little feeling or concern for Him. As He did with the disciples, Jesus also exhorts us to watch with Him by praying. However, the cure for our apathy comes not from praying, but from the Savior who suffered intensely and still wants His apathetic disciples.

BIBLE STUDY

1. Read Matthew 26:30–35. After they celebrate the Passover in the Upper Room, Jesus and His disciples go to the Mount of Olives. What does Jesus predict about all of His disciples? How does Peter respond, and what does Jesus predict about Peter in particular?

2. In Matthew 26:36, once they come to Gethsemane, what does Jesus tell His disciples to do, and what does He intend to do?

3. According to Matthew 26:37, Jesus takes Peter, James, and John—His closest disciples—with Him as He prays. For what other event did Jesus take these three aside (see Matthew 17:1–8)? What does He reveal to them in Matthew 17? What does He reveal to them in Matthew 26:37–38? Why is this important?

4. In Matthew 26:38, what does Jesus tell Peter, James, and John to do while He goes off to pray? How does Luke 22:40 explain what Jesus means by "watch"?

5. Read Matthew 26:39. What posture does Jesus take as He prays, and what does this mean? What does Jesus petition His Father to do for Him? What does He want even more than that? Notice how Jesus prays one of the very petitions that He taught His disciples (and us) to pray in Matthew 6:10. How does Jesus' prayer reveal both His humanity and His divinity?

6. To what "cup" does Jesus refer when He prays, "if it be possible, let this cup pass from Me" (Matthew 26:39)? See Psalm 75:8 and Isaiah 51:17. What other kind of "cup" does the Bible mention? See Psalm 23:5–6; 116:13; 1 Corinthians 10:16.

7. According to Matthew 26:40–41, what are Jesus' disciples doing when He returns from praying? How does this show their apathy during Jesus' intense suffering? What does Jesus exhort them to do? What does Jesus reveal about our human nature when we face trial and temptation?

8. In Matthew 26:42, how does Jesus pray this second time? How does this differ from His first prayer in 26:39?

9. Why do you think Jesus does not wake His disciples and exhort them to prayer in Matthew 26:43–44?

10. What details does Luke 22:43–44 add to highlight the intensity of Jesus' suffering?

11. Read Hebrews 5:7–10. What does this passage say about Jesus' prayers to the Father and how the Father answered the prayers of His Son? Based on this passage, how do we benefit from Jesus' intense suffering in Gethsemane?

12. In Matthew 26:45, what Gospel comfort can we find when we fall to the temptation of being apathetic toward Jesus and His intense suffering on our behalf?

CONCLUSION

Like the disciples in Gethsemane, we find it difficult to watch and pray constantly with our Lord Jesus, the Suffering Savior. Our lack of concern for Him and His suffering still wounds Him! However, in His great mercy and compassion, our Lord still serves as "the source of eternal salvation to all who obey Him" (Hebrews 5:9). He still heals us from our apathy, and He still wants us, just as He wanted the disciples.

LEADER

Midweek 3

THE WOUND OF APATHY

THEME VERSE

And [Jesus] said to Peter, "So, could you not watch with Me one hour? Watch and pray that you may not enter into temptation. The spirit indeed is willing, but the flesh is weak." (Matthew 26:40–41)

TEXT

Matthew 26:36–45

INTRODUCTION

When Jesus suffers the weight of the world's sin, He also suffers the wound of our apathy. The word *apathy* means "without feeling or concern." When the disciples fall asleep during Jesus' hour of intense suffering, they show little feeling or concern for Him. As He did with the disciples, Jesus also exhorts us to watch with Him by praying. However, the cure for our apathy comes not from praying, but from the Savior who suffered intensely and still wants His apathetic disciples.

BIBLE STUDY ANSWERS AND COMMENTARY

1. Jesus predicts that His disciples will fall away because of Him. They, the sheep, will be scattered when He, the shepherd, suffers and dies. However, their comfort lies in Jesus' resurrection (Matthew 26:32). Peter vows that he "will never fall away" (26:33), but Jesus knows how weak Peter's human nature (and ours) truly is. Thus He predicts that Peter will deny Him three times before the rooster crows (26:34).

2. In Matthew 26:36, Jesus tells His disciples to sit in one place while He goes to pray in another place. Surely, He wants privacy as He goes to face His intense suffering, but He does not want to be completely alone. According to Luke 22:40, Jesus asks the disciples not merely to sit but also to pray in order that they may not fall into temptation.

3. In Matthew 17:1–8, Jesus took Peter, James, and John with Him to the Mount of Transfiguration to reveal His divine glory as He conversed with Moses and Elijah about His suffering and death, His "departure" (Luke 9:31). In Matthew 26:37–38, Jesus takes the same three men and reveals His intense suffering to them. He wants their company and support as He begins "to be sorrowful and troubled." Why is this important? On the Mount of Transfiguration, Jesus reveals His glory; at Gethsemane, He reveals His suffering and grief. He shows His followers that His glory comes through suffering the wounds of our sin and death.

4. In Matthew 26:38, Jesus tells His closest disciples: "Remain here, and watch with Me." However, when He uses the word "watch," He does not mean "to be on guard." In Luke 22:40, Jesus says, "Pray that you may not enter into temptation." When Jesus says, "Watch," He means, "Pray!" In this way, the disciples would demonstrate their care and concern for their Master.

5. After Jesus leaves His closest disciples to watch and pray, He goes farther into the garden and falls down on His face to pray, thus showing deep humility and intense prayer. He now feels the weight of the world's sin and death being placed upon Him. Our Lord asks His Father to "let this cup pass from Me" (Matthew 26:39). However, He would rather do His Father's will. When Jesus prays, "Not as I will, but as You will," we hear Him praying the Third Petition of the Lord's Prayer (Matthew 6:10). Jesus shows His divinity as the Son who communes with and relies upon His heavenly Father, and He shows His humanity as He suffers the weight of the world's sin and death. In His humanity, Jesus wants to be free from the suffering, but in His divinity, He wants to do His Father's will.

6. Here in Gethsemane the "cup" refers to Jesus' impending suffering, crucifixion, and sleep in death. Psalm 75:7–8 refers to the "cup with foaming wine" of God's judgment upon the "wicked of the earth." In Isaiah 51:17, God's own people drink from "the cup of His wrath" when they stray from Him. However, Scripture also speaks of the "cup" of God's salvation—the cup that overflows with God's goodness and mercy (Psalm 23:5–6); "the cup of salvation" (Psalm 116:13), as we sing in the Offertory in the Divine Service; and the "cup of blessing," because it is "a participation in the blood of Christ" (1 Corinthians 10:16).

7. When Jesus returns from His first round of praying, He finds His disciples asleep. Their care and concern for Him in His sorrow had waned and grown cold. They show their apathy! Jesus then exhorts them: "Watch and pray that you may not enter into temptation" (Matthew 26:41). Whereas their sleeping betrayed their apathy, their watchful prayers would demonstrate their concern and loyalty for Him. However, Jesus knows the weakness of human nature: "The spirit indeed is willing, but the flesh is weak" (26:41). When we face times of trial and temptation, we are too weak to handle them alone, no matter how willing we think we may be.

8. In Matthew 26:42, Jesus prays, "My Father, if this cannot pass unless I drink it, Your will be done." No longer does He ask that the "cup" of His suffering be taken away (26:39). Now He prays that, since it cannot pass, the Father's will be done. The Father's will is that His Son bear the suffering, the sin, and the death of the world. Our Lord Jesus, the Son of God and perfect Man, submits to His Father's divine will.

9. These verses do not say why Jesus did not wake His disciples, and answers may vary. Perhaps the chief reason is that Jesus recognizes the weakness of their flesh, and He decides simply to bear and suffer their continued apathy as they sleep without concern for Him while His soul is very sorrowful, even to death.

10. Luke tells us that "an angel from heaven" (22:43) appears to strengthen Jesus during His time of intense sorrow. Luke also tells us that Jesus' intense praying and great sorrow has physical manifestations. Not only does Jesus sweat as He prays (which is intense by itself!), but "His sweat became like great drops of blood falling down to the ground" (22:44). Already in His prayers, Jesus sheds His blood as He bears the wounds of our apathy, sin, and death!

11. Hebrews 5:7–10 provides good commentary on Jesus' intense prayers in Gethsemane. He offered up His prayers "with loud cries and tears," and He "was heard because of His reverence." The Father heard His prayers and answered by saying, "Son, You may bear these wounds of the world's sin and death." Thus Jesus "learned obedience through what He suffered," and "He became the source of eternal salvation to all who obey Him." Jesus' sufferings, His intense prayers, and His obedience are the source of our salvation before God. Jesus suffered for our apathy, but we benefit from His great concern and prayerful vigil as He prepared to endure the cross for us.

12. Although Jesus suffered from the apathy of His disciples, He still wanted them to accompany Him as He was "betrayed into the hands of sinners" (Matthew 26:45). Their apathy did not disqualify them from being His disciples, because He is faithful to them. Despite our apathy, our lack of commitment, toward Jesus, He still wants us to benefit from His intense sorrow and suffering for us. Our apathy does not disqualify us from being His Christians; instead, He remains faithful to us in caring for us and healing us from sin and death.

Conclusion

Like the disciples in Gethsemane, we find it difficult to watch and pray constantly with our Lord Jesus, the Suffering Savior. Our lack of concern for Him and His suffering still wounds Him! However, in His great mercy and compassion, our Lord still serves as "the source of eternal salvation to all who obey Him" (Hebrews 5:9). He still heals us from our apathy, and He still wants us, just as He wanted the disciples.

STUDENT

Midweek 4

THE WOUND OF DENIAL

THEME VERSE

And the Lord turned and looked at Peter. And Peter remembered the saying of the Lord, how He had said to him, "Before the rooster crows today, you will deny Me three times." And he went out and wept bitterly. (Luke 22:61–62)

TEXT

Matthew 26:69–75

INTRODUCTION

Jesus has been wounded by Judas's betrayal and by the apathy of His disciples, but Peter's denial inflicts a wound even more painful. Peter's denial cuts deeper because he is one of Jesus' closest followers, and his denial is more intentional than apathy. Yet while Jesus suffers Peter's denial, and ours, He remains devoted to winning salvation and life with God for Peter and for us.

BIBLE STUDY

1. Read Matthew 26:34–35. What had Jesus predicted about Peter, and how did Peter respond?

2. For Peter's first denial of Jesus, read Matthew 26:69–70. What does the servant girl say to Peter? How does Peter deny Jesus the first time? Also read John 18:15–18 for more details of Peter's first denial. How did Peter get into the courtyard of the high priest?

77

3. For Peter's second denial of Jesus, read Matthew 26:71–72. What does the other servant girl say and to whom? How does Peter respond this time, and what does this mean?

4. For Peter's third denial of Jesus, read Matthew 26:73–74. Who confronts him now? How does Peter respond this third time, and what does it mean?

5. In Matthew 26:75, after the rooster crows, what does Peter remember? What does this cause him to do? Now read Luke 22:61–62. In this passage, what caused Peter to remember the Lord's words about his denial?

6. Read Matthew 5:16. What had Jesus taught Peter and all of His followers about living among other people? Now read Matthew 10:33. What had Jesus taught Peter and His other followers about denying Him before men? What does this suggest about Peter's threefold denial?

7. According to Matthew 26:75 (see also Mark 14:72 and Luke 22:62), Peter "went out and wept bitterly" after he realized what he had done. What does this bitter weeping show, and how does it differ from the remorse of Judas in Matthew 27:3–5?

8. How does the Lord Jesus pronounce His absolution for Peter's denial in Mark 16:7 and in John 21:15–17?

9. Read Acts 3:13–15. What kind of denial does Peter address as he preaches to the people gathered in Solomon's portico? How does Peter's denial of Jesus give credibility to his preaching in Acts 3:14–15?

10. In what ways do we deny our Lord Jesus Christ? How do Matthew 10:33 and 2 Timothy 2:13 help us take such denials seriously? What hope and comfort do we have when we are guilty of denying our Lord? See 2 Timothy 2:14; Acts 2:37–39, 42.

Conclusion

The wound of denial cuts deeper than other wounds we have studied so far. However, Jesus remains faithful even amid our denials, whether they are intentional or accidental. Our denial of Jesus certainly wounds Him, and He does not excuse such denials, but He does forgive them through His suffering, death, and resurrection. Because He suffered the wound of Peter's denial and suffers from our denials, He knows our weakness, but He also freely forgives and heals us from this wound. His forgiveness heals us to make the good confession of Him as Savior.

LEADER

Midweek 4

THE WOUND
OF DENIAL

THEME VERSE

And the Lord turned and looked at Peter. And Peter remembered the saying of the Lord, how He had said to him, "Before the rooster crows today, you will deny Me three times." And he went out and wept bitterly. (Luke 22:61–62)

TEXT

Matthew 26:69–75

INTRODUCTION

Jesus has been wounded by Judas's betrayal and by the apathy of His disciples, but Peter's denial inflicts a wound even more painful. Peter's denial cuts deeper because he is one of Jesus' closest followers, and his denial is more intentional than apathy. Yet while Jesus suffers Peter's denial, and ours, He remains devoted to winning salvation and life with God for Peter and for us.

BIBLE STUDY ANSWERS AND COMMENTARY

1. After Jesus announced that all of His disciples would forsake Him

(Matthew 26:31–32), Peter boldly vowed his allegiance. However, Jesus told Peter, "This very night, before the rooster crows, you will deny Me three times" (26:34). Peter, again boldly, asserted that he would not deny Jesus, even if he "must die" (26:35).

2. The first servant girl says, "You also were with Jesus the Galilean" (Matthew 26:69), thus highlighting Peter's association with Jesus. Peter, however, denies both Jesus and his personal connection to Him by saying, "I do not know what you mean" (26:70). Peter distances himself from Jesus, and he denies the Lord by feigning ignorance. John's Gospel tells us how Peter needed the assistance of "another disciple" (John) to enter the high priest's courtyard (18:15). This, no doubt, drew attention to Peter and led the servant girl to confront him.

3. The second servant girl draws more attention to Peter as she addresses the bystanders and says, "This man was with Jesus of Nazareth" (Matthew 26:71). She also highlights Peter's connection to Jesus. Peter, though, escalates his denial by using "an oath" and saying, "I do not know the man" (26:72). His initial feigned ignorance escalates to a sworn ignorance as he further disconnects himself from Jesus and claims that he does not know Him. Peter wants to protect himself by lying and denying, and because people in the courtyard do not believe his false claims, he feels he must invoke an oath. How he wounds both his Lord and his connection to Him!

4. In the third denial, the bystanders confront Peter by noting his Galilean accent and connecting him with the band of Jesus' followers. Although fearfully preoccupied with protecting himself, Peter's claims of ignorance cannot hide his accent. So Peter further escalates his denial: "He began to invoke a curse on himself and to swear, 'I do not know the man'" (Matthew 26:74). Now Peter feigns ignorance of Jesus both by swearing an oath and by calling a curse down on himself. In trying to preserve himself, Peter cuts himself off from the Lord Jesus. He also cuts himself off from Jesus' followers, His Church. Denying Jesus also involves denying His Body, the Church, and vice versa.

5. According to Matthew 26:75, as soon as the rooster crows, Peter remembers "the saying"—the word—of Jesus, when He said, "Before the rooster crows, you will deny Me three times." This word of Jesus leads Peter to realize how he has denied his Lord, but it also leads him to find solace and comfort in Jesus' words of mercy. Luke's Gospel adds another detail that caused Peter to remember the Lord's "saying": "The Lord turned and looked at Peter" (22:61–62), and it is this look that leads Peter to remember Jesus' words. Not only does this indicate that Peter could see Jesus while He was on trial, but it also shows that our Lord realizes when Peter inflicts Him with the wound of denial.

6. In Matthew 5:16, Jesus tells Peter and all of His followers, "Let your light shine before others, so that they may see your good works and give glory to your Father who is in heaven." That is, Jesus' followers confess, or acknowledge, Him and glorify His heavenly Father in their lives of good works. This serves as a stark contrast to Peter's denial of Jesus. In Matthew 10:33, as He sends out the Twelve, Jesus teaches Peter and the others: "Whoever denies Me before men, I also will deny before My Father who is in heaven." Peter should have known, therefore, that his denials of Jesus would result in Jesus denying him before the heavenly Father. The wound of denial is quite serious indeed!

7. When Peter leaves the courtyard and weeps bitterly, he shows repentance for his serious wound of denial that he inflicted upon Jesus. Not only had he feigned ignorance of Jesus, but he also took an oath before the bystanders and called down curses on himself, cutting himself off from Jesus and from his fellow believers. Peter's remembrance of the Lord's words led him to this bitter, tearful repentance. This differs from what happens with Judas. Judas also realized how he had betrayed "innocent blood." However, Judas did not repent of the wound he inflicted on Jesus; rather, he despaired and hanged himself.

8. Because Judas gave in to despair and hanged himself, he did not have the opportunity to savor the mercy and forgiveness of Jesus. Peter, though, did savor the Lord's absolution, as we see in the resurrection accounts. In Mark 16:7, the young man (angel) at the empty tomb of Jesus announces the Lord's resurrection and instructs the women to "go, tell His disciples *and Peter* that He is going before you to Galilee" (*emphasis added*). Peter is singled out because he had denied Jesus and because he would be especially comforted by the Lord's resurrection forgiveness and healing. In John 21:15–17, we read how the risen Lord applies the healing of His resurrection forgiveness to Peter: Jesus gives a threefold absolution for Peter's threefold denial.

9. Peter is not the only one to deny Jesus in His Passion. In Acts 3:13–15, Peter confronts the people in Jerusalem with the fact that they also denied Jesus "in the presence of Pilate, when he had decided to release Him." They "denied the Holy and Righteous One" and "killed the Author of life, whom God raised from the dead." However, Peter's denial does not diminish his message of the Lord's forgiveness and mercy. Rather, Peter stands uniquely qualified to speak of such denial, not only because he inflicted this wound on his Lord but also because His Lord had already forgiven and restored him.

10. We deny our Lord in ways similar to Peter's denials: we feign ignorance when others ask us about Jesus; we distance ourselves from Him and His Church so as not to stand out from others. However, as Matthew 10:33 (discussed above) and 2 Timothy 2:12 remind us, such denial is very serious, because "if we deny Him, He also will deny us." However, when we deny our Lord and our association with Him, we do have hope and promised comfort. "If we are faithless, He remains faithful—for He cannot deny Himself" (2 Timothy 2:13). Just as the crowd in Acts 2:37 repented for denying and rejecting Jesus, we also can repent of our denials and receive the Lord's forgiveness in our Baptism (see Acts 2:38–39).

Conclusion

The wound of denial cuts deeper than other wounds we have studied so far. However, Jesus remains faithful even amid our denials, whether they are intentional or accidental. Our denial of Jesus certainly wounds Him, and He does not excuse such denials, but He does forgive them through His suffering, death, and resurrection. Because He suffered the wound of Peter's denial and suffers from our denials, He knows our weakness, but He also freely forgives and heals us from this wound. His forgiveness heals us to make the good confession of Him as Savior.

STUDENT

Midweek 5

THE WOUND
OF MOCKERY

THEME VERSE

So Jesus came out, wearing the crown of thorns and the purple robe. Pilate said to them, "Behold, the man!" (John 19:5)

TEXT

Matthew 27:27–31

INTRODUCTION

The old schoolyard chant says, "Sticks and stones can break my bones, but names will never hurt me." However, any student called a hurtful name would strongly disagree. Mocking words, as well as actions, greatly wound. In this lesson, we see how Jesus endures the wound of mockery at the hands of Roman soldiers. In their words and actions the soldiers make fun of the true King of the universe, and thus He bears the wounds of our mockery, both the wounds we endure and the wounds we inflict. We can thank our Lord for enduring the wound of mockery, because "with His stripes we are healed" (Isaiah 53:5).

BIBLE STUDY

1. Jesus had predicted His Passion in general and His mocking in particular. According to Matthew 20:17–19, what are the specific details of Jesus' prediction?

2. According to Matthew 26:47, at whose hands did Jesus suffer in the Garden of Gethsemane? At whose hands did He suffer in Matthew

83

26:57, 67–68? In Matthew 27:11–26, at whose hands does our Lord suffer? Now read Matthew 27:27–31. At whose hands does our Lord Jesus suffer in this passage? Putting these passages together, what does this mean?

3. What did the soldiers do to Jesus in Matthew 27:28? What is the significance of the scarlet robe? See also Mark 15:17; John 19:2; Isaiah 1:18. How does this element of the mocking of Jesus also hearken back to Exodus 26:1? See also John 2:18–22.

4. In Matthew 27:29, what is the significance of the crown of thorns and the reed placed in Jesus' right hand? See, for example, Genesis 49:10; 2 Samuel 5:1–4; 1 Timothy 6:15; and Revelation 14:14. How does this element of Jesus' mocking also point to Him as our priest who offers the perfect sacrifice to God? See Exodus 29:5–6 and Hebrews 9:24–28.

5. When the soldiers mock Jesus and say, "Hail, King of the Jews" (Matthew 27:29), why do they use this particular phrase? See verse 37 and John 19:19–22. For what reason do the soldiers inflict this wound of mockery on Jesus? What message does God reveal by this mockery?

6. How does our Lord Jesus fulfill Isaiah 50:6 as He suffers the wound of mockery?

7. Read Isaiah 53:3–7. How does our Lord's wound of mockery fulfill this prophecy? What does this passage say about our part in the mockery that our Lord suffered? According to Isaiah 53, how does the mocking of Jesus actually work to save us?

8. How do we Christians often share in the wound of our Lord's mockery? See Psalm 79:4 and Psalm 89:50.

9. When we Christians suffer mockery from non-Christians around us, what comfort can we gain from Romans 8:18 and 1 Peter 4:13?

Conclusion

The Roman soldiers certainly made fun of our Lord Jesus Christ as they wounded Him with mockery. However, our gracious God uses this hurtful event to show us our true King and Priest, our Savior who valiantly conquers our sin and death by offering Himself as the perfect sacrifice. While the words of insult and the actions of abuse certainly hurt Jesus, His suffering and death ensure that no amount of mockery can remove God's love, life, and forgiveness from us.

<u>L</u>EADER

Midweek 5

THE WOUND OF MOCKERY

THEME VERSE

So Jesus came out, wearing the crown of thorns and the purple robe. Pilate said to them, "Behold, the man!" (John 19:5)

TEXT

Matthew 27:27–31

INTRODUCTION

The old schoolyard chant says, "Sticks and stones can break my bones, but names will never hurt me." However, any student called a hurtful name would strongly disagree. Mocking words, as well as actions, greatly wound. In this lesson, we see how Jesus endures the wound of mockery at the hands of Roman soldiers. In their words and actions the soldiers make fun of the true King of the universe, and thus He bears the wounds of our mockery, both the wounds we endure and the wounds we inflict. We can thank our Lord for enduring the wound of mockery, because "with His stripes we are healed" (Isaiah 53:5).

BIBLE STUDY ANSWERS AND COMMENTARY

1. In Matthew 20:17–19, our Lord predicts and outlines the wounds of His Passion. The Jewish leaders would condemn Him to death and deliver Him over to the Gentiles, and the Gentiles would mock Him, flog Him, and crucify Him. In Jesus' Passion, everything, including the mocking, proceeds according to His divine plan.

2. When Jesus is arrested (Matthew 26:47), He suffers at the hands of "a great crowd with swords and clubs, from the chief priests and the elders of the people," that is, at the hands of common Jewish people. When Jesus suffers the mock trial before the Jewish council (26:57, 67–68), He suffers at the hands of the Jewish ruling elite. When Jesus stands trial before Pontius Pilate (27:11–16), He suffers at the hands of the Roman (Gentile) ruling class. And when the Roman soldiers mock Him (27:27–31), He suffers at the hands of common Roman citizens. Putting these references together, we see how Jesus suffers at the hands of *all people*—the Jews and the Gentiles, the ruling elite and the common folk.

3. In Matthew 27:28, the Roman soldiers strip Jesus and put a scarlet robe on Him. Mark 15:17 and John 19:2 use the term "purple" robe, which means the same thing. The scarlet/purple robe is a symbol of kingly authority. The Roman emperor or another king might wear a robe of such color. When we remember Isaiah 1:18, we also see great theological significance: "Though [our] sins are like scarlet, they shall be white as snow." In His bitter Passion, our Lord Jesus is clothed with our sins, which are like scarlet. The color scarlet also reminds us of the Old Testament tabernacle (Exodus 26:1), where God dwelt with His people Israel and forgave their sins through the blood of sacrifices. We can recall how Jesus referred to "the temple of His body" (John 2:21) when He predicted His Passion, death, and resurrection.

4. When the soldiers mockingly place a crown of thorns on Jesus' head and a reed in His right hand, they give Him the appearance of a king, albeit a sad-looking one. Yet for us Christians, this is our true King! Genesis 49:10 speaks of the scepter and ruler's staff that will not depart from Judah and his descendants. Second Samuel 5:1–4 relates the anointing of David as king of Israel. Both of these passages are now fulfilled in the King who wears a mock crown and carries a mock scepter, because He is the "only Sovereign, the King of kings and Lord of lords" (1 Timothy 6:15). The mock crown and scepter will give way to "a golden crown on His head, and a sharp sickle in His hand" (Revelation 14:14) in His eternal victory over sin and death. Again, the mockery points us to Jesus as the perfect sacrifice for our sin and death. In Exodus 29:5–6, the high priest wore "the turban on his head" and "the holy crown on the turban," and Hebrews 9:24–28 indicates that Jesus is our High Priest who "has appeared once for all at the end of the ages to put away sin by the sacrifice of Himself." Even as Jesus is wounded by mockery, we still see Him as our holy King and Priest.

5. The soldiers use the very words of Jesus' indictment. Matthew 27:37 tells us that once Jesus is upon the cross, "over His head they put the charge against Him, which read, 'This is Jesus, the King of the Jews.'" John 19:19–22 phrases the charge "Jesus of Nazareth, King of the Jews" and indicates that Pilate inscribed the indictment in Aramaic, Latin, and Greek for all to read. The Roman soldiers use the words of the indictment to make fun of Jesus, but God uses this scorn to reveal His ultimate truth: Jesus is "King of the Jews," that is, King of His holy, redeemed people.

6. Isaiah 50:6 says, "I gave My back to those who strike, and My cheeks to those who pull out the beard; I hid not My face from disgrace and spitting." We need not pity Jesus as He suffers the wound of mockery nor should we view Him as the hapless victim. Instead, our Lord willingly placed Himself in the hands of the mockers. He gave Himself to those who cruelly abused Him. He did not hide or shrink from the disgrace and spitting of the soldiers, whose sole intent was to make fun of Him with bitterness and scorn. Jesus identified Himself with the Suffering Servant of Isaiah and thus accomplished our salvation.

7. As we ponder Jesus' wound of mockery, we also remember the prophecy of Isaiah 53:3 7. Our Lord is despised and rejected by men; He is acquainted with grief; He is despised while we, the human race, esteem Him not; He is oppressed and afflicted, yet He does not open His mouth to defend Himself or complain. As Isaiah also indicates, *we* are the ones who inflict such painful mockery on the Lord of life because "He was wounded for our transgressions; He was crushed for our iniquities" (53:5). However, this mocking serves God's saving purpose, because "upon Him was the chastisement that brought us peace, and with His stripes we are healed" (53:5).

8. Because we Christians are joined to Christ's death and resurrection in our Baptism (see Romans 6:1–4), we also suffer with Him in being mocked by the world. "We have become a taunt to our neighbors, mocked and derided by those around us" (Psalm 79:4). We cry out to our loving Lord: "Remember, O Lord, how Your servants are mocked, and how I bear in my heart the insults of all the many nations" (Psalm 89:50).

9. When we Christians are mocked for being joined to Christ Jesus, we need not despair. Instead, we take upon our lips and into our hearts the words of St. Paul: "the sufferings of this present time are not worth comparing with the glory that is to be revealed to us" (Romans 8:18). St. Peter also gives comfort and hope when he exhorts: "Rejoice insofar as you share Christ's sufferings, that you may also rejoice and be glad when His glory is revealed" (1 Peter 4:13). When we are mocked by the unbelieving world, we have the hope and joy of Christ's eternal victory over sin and death.

CONCLUSION

The Roman soldiers certainly made fun of our Lord Jesus Christ as they wounded Him with mockery. However, our gracious God uses this hurtful event to show us our true King and Priest, our Savior who valiantly conquers our sin and death by offering Himself as the perfect sacrifice. While the words of insult and the actions of abuse certainly hurt Jesus, His suffering and death ensure that no amount of mockery can remove God's love, life, and forgiveness from us.

STUDENT

Midweek 6

THE WOUND
OF ABANDONMENT

THEME VERSE

And about the ninth hour Jesus cried out with a loud voice, saying, "Eli, Eli, lema sabachthani?" that is, "My God, My God, why have You forsaken Me?" (Matthew 27:46)

TEXT

Matthew 27:45–48

INTRODUCTION

Our Lord Jesus has suffered wounds inflicted by fallen, sinful human beings: betrayal by Judas, apathy from His disciples, denial by Peter, and mockery from Roman soldiers. Is it possible for our Lord to suffer at the hands of God His Father? Not only has our Lord suffered the wound of abandonment from His fellow human beings, but He also suffers abandonment from His heavenly Father. However, this wound of abandonment heals our alienation from God. Our Lord's abandonment on the cross rescues us from our sin and death and restores us to life with God.

BIBLE STUDY

1. Matthew 27:45 gives us the first time reference for the events of Good Friday in Matthew's account. What additional time reference does Mark 15:25 give? How do these time references correlate to our modern reckoning of time? What is the timeline of Jesus' crucifixion to this point?

89

2. Read Zechariah 13:7; Matthew 26:31–32; and John 16:32. How had Jesus predicted His abandonment by His disciples?

3. As Jesus hangs on the cross, "there was darkness over all the land" (Matthew 27:45). What does "darkness" mean beyond the obvious physical phenomenon? See Deuteronomy 5:22–24; Psalm 18:7–12; 107:10–14; Proverbs 4:19; Amos 5:20; Zephaniah 1:15; John 12:46; and 2 Corinthians 4:6.

4. According to Matthew 27:46, Jesus cries out in a loud voice and quotes from Psalm 22: "My God, My God, why have You forsaken Me?" How can we hear Jesus lamenting His abandonment by God? How can we hear Him also crying out in faith?

5. Read Psalm 22. How does this psalm predict our Lord's suffering and abandonment? Concentrate on verses 1–2, 6–8, 14–18. How does this psalm reveal our Lord's hope and trust in God's presence and deliverance for Him? See verses 3–5, 9–11, 19–26.

6. According to Psalm 22:27–31, what results come out of Jesus' trust in God amid His experience of abandonment by God?

7. How can we say that God the Father abandoned His Son as He died on the cross?

8. Read Matthew 27:47–48. What did the bystanders hear when Jesus called out to God? What does this tell us about their expectation? Why does one of them offer a sponge soaked in sour wine for Jesus to drink? See Psalm 69:21 and Matthew 25:35.

9. How does Jesus' abandonment by God work for our salvation? See 2 Corinthians 5:21.

10. When we feel abandoned by God, what hope and comfort can we find in Psalm 13; Matthew 28:20; and Hebrews 13:5?

Conclusion

In His human nature Jesus suffered the wound of abandonment, complete with feelings of despair and loneliness. He suffered the very separation from God that we suffer as a result of our sin. However, the

Son of God did not give in to despair because, as the Son of God, He also remained completely united with His heavenly Father. With His experience of abandonment and His cry of despair, our Lord Jesus reconciles and reunites us with our loving God. Jesus' abandonment puts an end to our alienation from God. Because Jesus suffered the wound of abandonment caused by our sin, we need never fear that God will abandon us. After all, He has promised, "I will never leave you nor forsake you" (Hebrews 13:5).

Leader

Midweek 6

The Wound of Abandonment

Theme Verse

And about the ninth hour Jesus cried out with a loud voice, saying, "Eli, Eli, lema sabachthani?" that is, "My God, My God, why have You forsaken Me?" (Matthew 27:46)

Text

Matthew 27:45–48

Introduction

Our Lord Jesus has suffered wounds inflicted by fallen, sinful human beings: betrayal by Judas, apathy from His disciples, denial by Peter, and mockery from Roman soldiers. Is it possible for our Lord to suffer at the hands of God His Father? Not only has our Lord suffered the wound of abandonment from His fellow human beings, but He also suffers abandonment from His heavenly Father. However, this wound of abandonment heals our alienation from God. Our Lord's abandonment on the cross rescues us from our sin and death and restores us to life with God.

BIBLE STUDY ANSWERS AND COMMENTARY

1. Matthew says that darkness came over the land from the sixth hour until the ninth hour—from about 12 noon until about 3 p.m. Mark 15:25 says, "It was the third hour when they crucified Him," that is, about 9 a.m. Putting these verses together into a timeline, Jesus is crucified at about 9 a.m., darkness descends over the land at about 12 noon, and Jesus dies at about 3 p.m.

2. Jesus' wound of abandonment was no accident. Five centuries earlier, our Lord predicted His abandonment by His disciples through the prophet Zechariah: "Strike the shepherd, and the sheep will be scattered" (13:7). Jesus cites this verse when He tells His disciples, "You will all fall away because of Me this night" (Matthew 26:31). Jesus also told them: "Behold, the hour is coming, indeed it has come, when you will be scattered, each to his own home, and will leave Me alone" (John 16:32).

3. Of course, "darkness over all the land" (Matthew 27:45) refers to the physical phenomenon of the sun failing to give its light (see Luke 23:45). However, darkness also has theological meaning. Deuteronomy 5:22–24 mentions "the cloud, and the thick darkness" when God descended to Mount Sinai to make His covenant with His people. Psalm 18:7–12 connects darkness with God's just wrath. Psalm 107:10–14 connects darkness with the "shadow of death" and says that God's salvation means rescuing us from death. Proverbs 4:19 compares the way of wickedness with darkness. Amos 5:20 and Zephaniah 1:15 connect darkness with "the day of the LORD" when He comes to judge the world with justice. In John 12:46, Jesus refers to unbelief as "darkness." Finally, 2 Corinthians 4:6 says that God's light brings us out of darkness (unbelief) into "the light of the knowledge of the glory of God in the face of Jesus Christ." Darkness refers to God's awesome presence, especially when He comes to judge the world for its unbelief. It also refers to wickedness and unbelief. All these meanings converge in Jesus' crucifixion. God is present, dying on the cross, while evil people abuse and abandon Him. God judges people for their rejection of His Son, yet in this cross we see the light of God's truth of forgiveness and life, which scatters the darkness of our unbelief.

4. At first we hear the words of Psalm 22 as Jesus expressing His experience of being abandoned even by His heavenly Father. Jesus' words express His despair because, in His humanity, He experiences the separation from God that we human beings have caused. However, Jesus also quotes Psalm 22 in faith, even amid experiencing abandonment. When Jesus says, "My God, My God," He shows that faith believes God even when He seems to be absent. Jesus calls on His Father in faith, though His experience tells Him that His Father is not there.

5. Psalm 22 predicts our Lord's abandonment by asking why God has forsaken Him and why He is so far from Him (verses 1–2). Verses 6–8 predict our Lord being mocked by people. Verses 14–18 predict our Lord's experience of utter physical torture and humiliation. However, Psalm 22 also reveals our Lord's hope and trust in God's deliverance. Although He experiences abandonment, Jesus still confesses God as holy and the one to be trusted (verses 3–5). He recognizes that the God who gave Him life in the Virgin's womb is not far from Him (verses 9–11). And He can still rely on His Father's deliverance and thus proclaim and glorify His name (verses 19–26).

6. Because Jesus experienced our separation from God, yet was delivered by Him, "all the ends of the earth shall remember and turn to the Lord, and all the families of the nations shall worship before [God]" (Psalm 22:27). Because Jesus was abandoned by both men and God, people will worship the God who always loves and is always present (verses 29–30), and "they shall come and proclaim His righteousness to a people yet unborn, that He has done it" (verse 31). Because Jesus suffered our separation from God, we are restored to the Father through the Son.

7. It seems like a contradiction that God, who is present everywhere, is absent from His Son as He hangs on the cross. How can God, who is love, turn His back on His own eternal Son? When Jesus says, "My God, My God, why have You forsaken Me?" He shows that, in His human nature, He truly experiences our human despair and separation from God that results from sin. However, as the Son of God, in His divine nature, He is not separated from His Father, because God is one and cannot be divided. Jesus still cries out in faith to His Father. When our Lord suffers our alienation from God in His humanity, He restores us who are estranged from God by our sin to true life with God.

8. When Jesus cries out, "Eli, Eli," the bystanders mistake Him to say, "Elijah, Elijah," and they want to see if the well-known prophet will intervene to help Him. They do not expect God's help; they mistakenly expect help from one of God's faithful servants. When one person offers a wine-soaked sponge to Jesus, he fulfills the prophecy of Psalm 69:21 and shows great charity in offering a drink to the One who thirsts (see Matthew 25:35).

9. Jesus' wound of abandonment means that we are reconciled to God, because "for our sake He [the Father] made Him [the Son] to be sin who knew no sin, so that in Him we might become the righteousness of God" (2 Corinthians 5:21). Jesus suffers our sinful separation from God in order to restore us and make us at one ("atonement") with God.

10. When we feel and experience abandonment by, or separation from, God, we can trust God and call upon Him amid our despair. Psalm 13 first expresses despair that God forgets and hides His face (verses 1–2), but then concludes with trust and rejoicing in God's salvation (verses 5–6). In Matthew 28:20, Jesus promises, "I am with you always, to the end of the age." Hebrews 13:5 comforts us with God's promise: "I will never leave you nor forsake you." Because Jesus suffered our wound of abandonment and separation from God, we can rely on God's promise that He will never leave us and that He will always be with us.

Conclusion

In His human nature Jesus suffered the wound of abandonment, complete with feelings of despair and loneliness. He suffered the very separation from God that we suffer as a result of our sin. However, the Son of God did not give in to despair because, as the Son of God, He also remained completely united with His heavenly Father. With His experience of abandonment and His cry of despair, our Lord Jesus reconciles and reunites us with our loving God. Jesus' abandonment puts an end to our alienation from God. Because Jesus suffered the wound of abandonment caused by our sin, we need never fear that God will abandon us. After all, He has promised, "I will never leave you nor forsake you" (Hebrews 13:5).

STUDENT

Easter Sunday

HE IS RISEN!
THE WOUND OF DEATH
IS VANQUISHED!

THEME VERSE

Then comes the end, when He delivers the kingdom to God the Father after destroying every rule and every authority and power. For He must reign until He has put all His enemies under His feet. The last enemy to be destroyed is death. (1 Corinthians 15:24–26)

TEXT

John 20:11–16

INTRODUCTION

Our Lord Jesus Christ has suffered the wounds of betrayal, apathy, denial, mockery, and abandonment— the very wounds that humanity inflicted upon itself by forsaking God in the Garden of Eden, wounds symptomatic of our slavery to sin and death. However, Christ is risen! He has conquered death! In His victorious resurrection He brings life and immortality to light for us. In conquering our last enemy, death, our Lord Jesus gives us eternal peace with God and eternal healing from the wounds of our sin.

BIBLE STUDY

1. Read John 20:11–16. Why did Mary first go to the tomb of Jesus? See John 20:1 and Mark 16:1. According to John 20:1–10, what event

95

precedes the event of our text? What message did the folded cloth that had covered Jesus' face give to Peter and John (20:7)?

2. As Mary stays behind at the empty tomb, she sees two angels inside the tomb. In John 20:13, what lament does Mary speak? According to Luke 24:4–7, what message do the angels give to her?

3. What might account for Mary's inability to recognize the risen Jesus in John 20:14–16? For whom does Mary mistake Him? What leads her to recognize Jesus? How does Mary show that she finally recognizes Jesus?

4. For a similar event with two other disciples, see Luke 24:15–16. What accounts for the inability of the disciples to recognize the risen Lord? How did the Emmaus disciples come to realize that they had conversed with Jesus? See Luke 24:30–31, 35.

5. Today's story is the first of four postresurrection appearances by the risen Lord recorded in John's Gospel. For the other appearances, see John 20:19–23; 20:26–29; and 21:1–14. In each appearance, to whom does the risen Lord reveal Himself, and what unique things does He do to include His followers in His resurrection life?

6. Read the following Old Testament passages that prepare us for our Lord's resurrection victory over death: Job 19:23–27; Psalm 68:1–3, 19–20; Isaiah 25:6–9. How does each passage predict and proclaim the Lord's victory over our last enemy, death?

7. How did our Lord Jesus proclaim in the following passages that He had come to defeat death itself: Matthew 4:16; John 5:24; John 11:25–26?

8. According to Romans 6:3–11; John 6:54; 2 Timothy 1:10; and 1 John 3:14, how do we now participate in and show forth Christ's victory over death?

9. What does 1 Corinthians 15:20–23 say about how and when we will fully enjoy Christ's victory over death for us?

10. Read the following passages to see how Jesus prepared us for the healing that comes from and in His resurrection: Matthew 4:23; 9:35; Acts 10:38; Revelation 22:1–3.

CONCLUSION

Despite suffering the wounds of our sin and death, wounds that sent Him to the cross and grave, our Lord Jesus Christ rose victorious on the third day. In His resurrection, our last enemy, the wound of death, has been defeated, now and for all eternity. In the Gospel and in Baptism, our Lord gives us the healing of His death and resurrection. When He comes again on the Last Day, we will fully enjoy His resurrection healing for all eternity.

LEADER

Easter Sunday

HE IS RISEN! THE WOUND OF DEATH IS VANQUISHED!

THEME VERSE

Then comes the end, when He delivers the kingdom to God the Father after destroying every rule and every authority and power. For He must reign until He has put all His enemies under His feet. The last enemy to be destroyed is death. (1 Corinthians 15:24–26)

TEXT

John 20:11–16

INTRODUCTION

Our Lord Jesus Christ has suffered the wounds of betrayal, apathy, denial, mockery, and abandonment—the very wounds that humanity inflicted upon itself by forsaking God in the Garden of Eden, wounds symptomatic of our slavery to sin and death. However, Christ is risen! He has conquered death! In His victorious resurrection He brings life and immortality to light for us. In conquering our last enemy, death, our Lord Jesus gives us eternal peace with God and eternal healing from the wounds of our sin.

Bible Study Answers and Commentary

1. Mary stands outside the tomb, weeping. However, John 20:1 indicates that she had been at the tomb earlier in the morning, "while it was still dark." Mary had been among the women who went to Jesus' tomb "so that they might go and anoint Him" (Mark 16:1). After she had visited the tomb, Mary ran back to tell the disciples that Jesus' tomb was empty (John 20:2). Peter and John ran to the tomb to see this sight. When they discovered the face cloth of Jesus "folded up in a place by itself" (John 20:1–10, especially verse 7), they realized that Jesus had risen, just as He had promised.

2. Mary returns to the tomb with, or after, Peter and John. Now she looks inside the tomb and sees two angels dressed in white. Mary laments, "They have taken away my Lord, and I do not know where they have laid Him" (John 20:13). Luke 24:5–7 gives the angels' message to Mary: "Why do you seek the living among the dead? He is not here, but has risen."

3. Mary is distracted from her conversation with the angels and turns to see someone else standing there, but she does not recognize this person as Jesus. Certainly Mary's tear-filled eyes and state of grief prevented her from recognizing the risen Christ, but Jesus also reveals Himself in His chosen ways. At first, Mary mistakes Jesus for the gardener who would tend the area around the tomb (John 20:15), but then Jesus reveals Himself by speaking Mary's name (verse 16). At this, Mary's grief turns to joy, and she cries out, "Rabboni!"—a term that shows devotion and respect, as in "dear Teacher."

4. The two Emmaus disciples do not recognize the risen Lord because "their eyes were kept from recognizing Him" (Luke 24:16). Again, Jesus reveals Himself in His chosen way: "When He was at table with them, He took the bread and blessed and broke it and gave it to them. And their eyes were opened, and they recognized Him" (Luke 24:30–31).

5. In John 20:19–23, Jesus reveals Himself on the evening of the first Easter to ten of the eleven disciples (see 20:24). Here Jesus breathes on the disciples, giving them His peace, the Holy Spirit, and the authority to forgive or retain sins. Jesus' victory over death means absolution for our sins. In John 20:26–29, Jesus reveals Himself one week later to all eleven disciples. He again gives them His peace, and He invites Thomas to touch His wounds and believe. However, Jesus commends "those who have not seen and yet have believed" (20:29), because for us Jesus' victory over death comes by faith. Finally, in John 21:1–14, Jesus reveals Himself when the disciples are fishing. After they catch a net full of fish, they recognize the risen Lord, and He prepares a meal for them. Our Lord reveals His victory over death and invites His followers to dine with Him, as He still does in Holy Communion.

6. Job predicted our Lord's resurrection by saying, "I know that my Redeemer lives . . . . And after my skin as been thus destroyed, yet in my flesh I shall see God" (19:25–26). Because Redeemer Jesus lives, we will see God in the flesh. Psalm 68 compares the risen Lord to a warrior who "shall arise, His enemies shall be scattered; and those who hate Him shall flee before Him" (verse 1). "The righteous shall be glad" (verse 3), because "our God is a God of salvation, and to God, the Lord, belong deliverances from death" (verse 20). Isaiah 25 compares Jesus' resurrection victory to a banquet of only the best food and wine. In Jesus' resurrection, God swallows up death forever, and the Lord God wipes away tears from all faces (Isaiah 25:8).

7. When Jesus began His ministry, He predicted His defeat over death when He said that "for those dwelling in the region and shadow of death, on them a light has dawned" (Matthew 4:16). During His ministry, Jesus said, "Whoever hears My word and believes Him who sent Me has eternal life" (John 5:24). Death is defeated when we hear our Lord's words. Just before He raised Lazarus, Jesus taught that believing in Him brings eternal life: "Whoever believes in Me, though he die, yet shall he live, and everyone who lives and believes in Me shall never die" (John 11:25–26).

8. According to Romans 6:3–11, we participate in Jesus' death and resurrection in our Baptism, dying to sin and rising to new life. According to John 6:54, we participate in Jesus' victory when we commune, because Jesus says that "whoever feeds on My flesh and drinks My blood has eternal life, and I will raise him up on the last day." Because our Lord has "abolished death and brought life and immortality to light through the gospel" (2 Timothy 1:10), we participate in His victory when we gladly hear and learn His Gospel. And we show forth this new life by loving our neighbors because "we know that we have passed out of death into life, because we love the brothers" (1 John 3:14).

9. While we participate in Christ's resurrection victory now by faith, we will realize and enjoy it fully on the Last Day. First Corinthians 15 identifies Jesus as "the firstfruits of those who have fallen asleep" (verse 20). The apostle Paul also writes: "In Christ shall all be made alive. But each in his own order: Christ the firstfruits, then at His coming those who belong to Christ" (1 Corinthians 15:22–23).

10. Jesus prepared us for His resurrection victory over death by "healing every disease and every affliction among the people" (Matthew 4:23; see also 9:35). According to Acts 10:38, Jesus "went about doing good and healing all who were oppressed by the devil." In His healings and in His resurrection, Jesus vanquishes the wound of death. We will fully realize this new life in eternity, when we will see "the river of the water of life" and "the tree of life with its twelve kinds of fruit, yielding its fruit each month. The leaves of the tree were for the healing of the nations" (Revelation 22:1–2).

CONCLUSION

Despite suffering the wounds of our sin and death, wounds that sent Him to the cross and grave, our Lord Jesus Christ rose victorious on the third day. In His resurrection, our last enemy, the wound of death, has been defeated, now and for all eternity. In the Gospel and in Baptism, our Lord gives us the healing of His death and resurrection. When He comes again on the Last Day, we will fully enjoy His resurrection healing for all eternity.

WORSHIP
RESOURCES

INTRODUCTION

The penitential season of Lent is also a catechetical season. Lenten catechesis may sometimes include a special focus on one or more of the Six Chief Parts of the Small Catechism, but it seeks a broader context. Lent is catechetical because it is pointing toward Baptism into the cross and resurrection of Christ. Historically, Lent developed as a season of preparation for Holy Baptism; liturgically and theologically, Lent is the Church's refocus on the significance of Holy Baptism. The daily drowning of contrition and repentance, which characterizes the entire Christian life of discipleship, is deliberately intensified during Lent as a renewal of faith and life in Christ. This repentance is never the product of human wisdom, reason, strength, or effort. Rather, it is always the divine work of the Holy Spirit through the Law and the Gospel. The Law crucifies the old Adam, and the Gospel raises up the new man in us. Thus a Lenten focus on the cross and Passion of the Lord Jesus Christ is not aimed at an emotional response, nor is it an appeal for greater effort or heroic self-sacrifice on the part of sinners. Rather, Lent is a pointed proclamation and confession of the Law and the Gospel, a preaching of repentance for the forgiveness of sins. Lent is properly penitential and most surely catechetical when it brings the cross to sinners and sinners to the cross of Christ as the fountain and source of forgiveness, life, and salvation.

The worship resources that follow have been prepared based on the hymn "O Sacred Head, Now Wounded" (*LSB* 450). Specific readings, psalmody, hymns, and prayers have been selected (along with appropriate options) with a view toward the special emphases of this series. At the same time, all these resources have been prepared on the foundation and within the context of the Church's traditional Lenten practices. For days such as Ash Wednesday, Good Friday, and Easter Sunday, the appointed propers have been respected, almost to a fault. The rites and rubrics of the official service books of The Lutheran Church—Missouri Synod have been followed. There is both wisdom and integrity in using that which has been received, and there is also the salutary benefit of catholicity in such a unified confession and practice of the faith.

The working assumption of this worship resource has been the availability of *Lutheran Service Book* (Concordia, 2006). The Orders of Matins (see the accompanying CD-ROM) and Vespers have been followed for the daily prayer offices, and Setting Three has been followed in the case of the Divine Service throughout Lent and Holy Week. The use of Setting One or Two has been suggested for the Divine Service on Easter Sunday. All of the suggested hymns can be found in *Lutheran Service Book.*

The more general liturgical practices of Lent and Holy Week are assumed and taken into account, but they are not necessarily specified in connection with each of the particular services of this Lenten series. For the sake of clarity, some of these traditional practices are as follows:

- The Alleluia is not sung from Ash Wednesday until the Easter Vigil.

- The Gloria in Excelsis is omitted from the Divine Service, even on the Sundays in Lent (though these Sundays are festivals in their own right and are not counted in the forty days *of* Lent). Exceptions to this omission of the Gloria in Excelsis are the festivals of St. Joseph, the Guardian of Jesus (March 19), and the Annunciation of Our Lord (March 25), as well as Holy (Maundy) Thursday.

- The Gloria Patri (the lesser Gloria) is not used during Holy Week, including the daytime services of Holy Thursday.

- Depending on local custom, the organ is not played during Lent except to accompany the singing of the congregation. Likewise, other instruments are silenced, including the ringing of bells in the service.

- Crosses throughout the church may be veiled with unbleached linen or violet cloth throughout Lent, though there are differences of opinion as to the significance of this practice and how (or if) it ought to be done. Where crosses are veiled, it is done with penitential reverence and humility, not for the sake of hiding or forgetting the cross (may it never be!). The intent of this practice is to increase the longing of the faithful for the cross. Local circumstance and pastoral discernment will determine how best to handle such a practice. For example, the processional cross may be unveiled for the services of Holy Week, beginning with the procession of palms on Passion Sunday. The veil of the altar cross may be changed to white for the Maundy Thursday Divine Service, and then the cross may be removed altogether at the stripping of the altar.

- Another local custom is the choice not to place flowers on the altar (or anywhere in the church) from Ash Wednesday until the Easter Vigil.

- In brief, there is comprehensive restraint of celebration while waiting and hungering for the Paschal Feast.

- In those congregations that use the Paschal candle, the candle remains in its place at the baptismal font and is used at baptisms and funerals during Lent and Holy Week.

Accompanying the restraint of celebration, and serving the catechetical purpose of the Lenten season, it is well to emphasize, teach, and encourage the practice of individual confession and absolution during Lent. Certainly, pastors ought to provide and publicize opportunities for this means of grace and forgiveness (if not throughout the year, then all the more so in this most penitential season). Along with that, it may be helpful to hold a Service of Corporate Confession and Absolution (see *Lutheran Service Book*, pp. 290–91) not only on Ash Wednesday and Holy (Maundy) Thursday but also at other times in the course of the season. Regrettably, many Lutherans have come to identify "confession and absolution" exclusively with the rites of preparation in connection with the Divine Service. Those rites have their place and serve their salutary purpose, but they were a relatively late addition to the liturgical practice of the Church, and they do not adequately take the place or provide the benefit of individual confession and absolution. It is recommended that during Lent the so-called "declaration of grace" (the right-hand column in the settings of the Divine Service, as for example on pp. 184–85 of *Lutheran Service Book*) be used in the rites of preparation instead of the indicative-active "I forgive you." Historically, the "declaration of grace" was by far the more common practice in this context among Lutherans and is less easily confused with the absolution of individual confession (from which the indicative-active form derives).

The following are the specific worship resources provided. (Please see the accompanying CD-ROM for additional worship resources for Passion Sunday and Holy Week.)

- **Ash Wednesday**: order of service, propers, notes, and rubrics, including suggestions for the imposition of ashes.

- **Lenten services**: Orders of service for daily prayer offices (Matins, which is on the accompanying CD-ROM, and/or

Vespers) and for midweek celebration of Holy Communion (Divine Service, Setting Three), with a full complement of propers for each service during the weeks of Lent.

- **Maundy Thursday**: Order of service, propers, notes, and rubrics, including suggestions for the Service of Corporate Confession and Absolution, the transition from Lent to the Triduum, and the stripping of the altar at the conclusion of the Divine Service.

- **Good Friday**: Order of service, propers, notes, and rubrics, including comments and suggestions on the adoration of the cross and the celebration of Holy Communion.

- **Easter Vigil:** Order of service, propers, notes, and rubrics, including an extended discussion of the theology and practice of the Vigil in its liturgical context.

- **Easter Sunday**: Order of service, propers, notes, and rubrics, including comments and suggestions on the various settings of the Divine Service.

- Choral and instrumental resources for the church musician.

Of course, in the interest of the free course and clarity of the Gospel, it is expected that pastors and congregations will adapt these worship resources according to their local circumstances. Respecting tradition and gratefully receiving that which has been given from the Lord through His Church on earth, the basic rule of liturgical practice is to be reverent and courteous, which is simply another way of describing faith toward God and fervent love toward one another. Therefore the following resources are listed to encourage a thoughtful examination of the historical, theological, and liturgical aspects of Lent, Holy Week, the Triduum, and the Feast of the Resurrection of Our Lord.

Resources

Adam, Adolf. *The Liturgical Year: Its History and Its Meaning after the Reform of the Liturgy*. Translated by Matthew J. O'Connell. New York, NY: Pueblo Publishing Company, 1981.

Bobb, Barry L., and Hans Boehringer. *Proclaim: A Guide for Planning Liturgy and Music*. 2d edition. St. Louis: Concordia, 1995.

Commission on Worship, the LCMS. *Lutheran Service Book: Altar Book*. St. Louis: Concordia, 2006.

Days of the Lord: The Liturgical Year. Volume 2: *Lent*. Volume 3: *Easter Triduum*. Collegeville, MN: Liturgical Press, 1993.

Lang, Paul H. D. *Ceremony and Celebration*. Especially chapter 17: "The Ceremonies of the Church Year, Part II: The Easter Season." St. Louis: Concordia, 1965. Repr.: Fort Wayne, IN: Redeemer Lutheran Church, 2004.

Lindemann, Fred H. *The Sermon and the Propers*. Volume 2: *Pre-Lent to Pentecost*. St. Louis: Concordia, 1958.

Nocent, Adrien. *The Liturgical Year*. Volume 2: *Lent*. Volume 3: *The Paschal Triduum, The Easter Season*. Translated by Matthew J. O'Connell. Collegeville, MN: Liturgical Press, 1977.

Parsch, Pius. *The Church's Year of Grace*. Volume 2: *Septuagesima to Holy Saturday*. Volume 3: *Easter to Pentecost*. 2d edition. Translated by Daniel Francis Coogan Jr. and Rudolph Kraus. Collegeville, MN: Liturgical Press, 1953.

Pfatteicher, Philip H. *Commentary on the* Lutheran Book of Worship*: Lutheran Liturgy in Its Ecumenical Context*. Especially pages 223–91. Minneapolis: Augsburg Fortress, 1990.

———, and Carlos R. Messerli. *Manual on the Liturgy: Lutheran Book of Worship*. Especially chapter 8: "Celebrating the Cross and Resurrection." Minneapolis: Augsburg, 1979.

Talley, Thomas J. *The Origins of the Liturgical Year*. 2d edition. Collegeville, MN: Liturgical Press, 1991.

Ash Wednesday

A Wounded Savior for a Wounded People

Imposition of Ashes/Confession and Absolution
(morning or afternoon/evening)

The congregation and pastor(s) enter in silence.
Stand

Opening Address

Kneel/Stand
Silence for reflection

Ash Wednesday Litany

Sit

Imposition of Ashes

During the imposition of ashes, members of the congregation may meditate on Psalm 90 or other penitential psalms (Psalms 6, 32, 38, 51, 102, 130, 143).

Hymn: "Savior, When in Dust to Thee" (*LSB* 419)

Service of Corporate Confession and Absolution

Divine Service

Stand

Introit: Psalm 51:1–3, 6–8 (antiphon, Psalm 51:17)

Kyrie

Salutation and Collect of the Day

Sit

OLD TESTAMENT: Joel 2:12–19

GRADUAL: Hebrews 12:2

EPISTLE: 2 Corinthians 5:20b–6:10

Stand

VERSE: Joel 2:13b

HOLY GOSPEL: Matthew 6:1–6, 16–21

Sit

HYMN OF THE DAY: "From Depths of Woe I Cry to Thee"
(LSB 607)

SERMON

OFFERING

Stand

OFFERTORY

PRAYER OF THE CHURCH

O Lord our God, the Father of mercies, You have no pleasure in the death of the wicked, but desire that the wicked turn from their way and live. Out of Your infinite goodness, You have delivered up Your only-begotten Son to the death of the cross as a sacrifice for our sins. For His sake, remember not our ingratitude and indifference, but have mercy upon us and forgive us all our sins.

As Your dear Son was wounded for our transgressions and by His stripes we are healed, let us daily meditate upon His Passion with true repentance and sincere faith, that His death may be our life, His righteousness our salvation, His conflict our victory and everlasting peace. Replenish us with Your Holy Spirit that, loving You with our whole hearts, we may walk by faith according to Your Word, blameless in Your sight. Teach us to love one another, to bear one another's burdens, and so to fulfill the Law of Christ, who came not to be served but to serve and who gave His life as a ransom for many. Help us likewise to love our enemies and from our hearts to forgive everyone who trespasses against us. Let us follow the example of our Savior in patiently enduring the trials and afflictions of this present world, that, having suffered with Him, we may also be glorified with Him. For His sake hear all who cry to You in sorrow and distress, and deliver them according to their need and Your abundant mercy.

Bestow Your blessing upon the ministry of reconciliation. May the preaching of the cross become a message of peace and the very power of Your Gospel unto the ends of the earth, that all the nations may be delivered from the darkness of their sins and glorify Your gracious name with all Your saints in light. Grant courage and strength to the ministers of Your Word to preach Christ and Him Crucified, both in season and out of season, calling sinners to repentance and believers to rejoice in Your salvation. May the death of Your Son be our comfort in our last hour, and let us depart in peace to rise with Him to life everlasting; for He lives and reigns with You and the Holy Spirit, one God, now and forever.

C: Amen.

PREFACE

PROPER PREFACE

SANCTUS

LORD'S PRAYER

THE WORDS OF OUR LORD

PAX DOMINI

AGNUS DEI

Sit

DISTRIBUTION HYMNS

"All Mankind Fell in Adam's Fall" (*LSB* 562)
"O Sacred Head, Now Wounded" (*LSB* 450)
"Baptismal Waters Cover Me" (*LSB* 616)
"Lord Jesus, Think on Me" (*LSB* 610)

Stand

NUNC DIMITTIS

THANKSGIVING

Post-Communion Collect

Salutation and Benedicamus

Benediction

Closing Hymn: "Jesus, Grant That Balm and Healing"
(*LSB* 421)

NOTES FOR THE ASH WEDNESDAY SERVICE FOR THE WORSHIP PLANNER

Ash Wednesday marks the beginning of Lent and sets the tone of the season. It is a pointed call to repentance, which is to say that it is a return to the death and resurrection of Holy Baptism by way of confession and faith in the forgiveness of sins. Thus the imposition of ashes, from which the day receives its name, recalls both the mortality of sinful man and the redemption of Christ into which His followers have been baptized. This context of contrition and repentance, fully and firmly centered in the cross and resurrection of Christ Jesus, is the framework within which the Lenten fast is undertaken. A focus on Christ's Passion will not be chiefly an emotional or intellectual exercise, though both the intellect and the emotions are engaged by the Word and Spirit of God. Rather, in faith the Passion is approached as the very heart of the Gospel, which the Lord our Savior has accomplished for us and now bestows on us with His means of grace.

There is a liturgical connection between Ash Wednesday and Maundy Thursday. The penitential discipline begun on this day is resolved in the Lord's cleansing of His disciples, and the fasting of repentance is ended with the Lord's feeding of His disciples in Holy Communion. Of course, this cleansing and feeding occur also on Ash Wednesday and throughout Lent, but they come into special focus on Maundy Thursday at the beginning of the Paschal Triduum. On a seasonal level, one may think of the relationship between Ash Wednesday and Maundy Thursday as following the rhythmic pattern of each Divine Service: a liturgical progression from contrition and confession, through the catechesis of the Word, to the feasting of the Lord's Supper.

Ideally, the imposition of ashes may be done in the morning of Ash Wednesday, so that the entire day is spent in penitential contemplation of our sin and mortality in view of God's grace and forgiveness. The rite is best administered in connection with confession and absolution, lest the penitent simply be turned upon himself. If it is unreasonable to suppose that many members of the congregation will be able to avail themselves of such an opportunity in the morning, the imposition of ashes and corporate confession may be repeated in the late afternoon or early evening, prior to the Divine Service.

The color of the day is violet (or black). The pastor(s) may prefer to wear cassock and surplice for the imposition of ashes and the Service of Corporate Confession and Absolution, but alb (and chasuble) for the Divine Service.

- The Imposition of Ashes is taken from *Lutheran Service Book: Altar Book*, 483–86. If the imposition of ashes is not used, the service begins with the Service of Corporate Confession and Absolution.

- The Ash Wednesday Litany is found on pages 484–85 of *Lutheran Service Book: Altar Book*. The Litany on pages 288–89 of *Lutheran Service Book*, concluding with the collect for Ash Wednesday, may be used instead.

- The actual imposition of ashes may be done in silence, without any instrumental or choral background.

- An alternate choice for the hymn after the imposition of ashes is "Lord, to You I Make Confession" (*LSB* 608).

- The Service of Corporate Confession and Absolution is found on pages 290–91 of *Lutheran Service Book* (pages 422–24 of *Lutheran Service Book: Altar Book*).

- If the imposition of ashes and the Service of Corporate Confession and Absolution take place in the morning or at a time significantly prior to the Divine Service, the pastor(s) and congregation leave in silence. If the Divine Service follows these two orders within a short period of time or immediately, a period of silence should be allowed before proceeding with the Introit Psalmody. The pastor(s) may use this time to change from cassock and surplice to alb. The celebrant of the Divine Service may also be vested in a chasuble at this point.

- This service is based on Setting Three of the Divine Service in *Lutheran Service Book*.

- The Offering may be received in silence while the altar is prepared for Holy Communion.

- The Offertory ("Create in me") may be sung as the Offering is presented at the altar, or it may precede the Offering, immediately following the Sermon.

- The Prayer of the Church has been adapted from pages 343–44 of *The Lutheran Liturgy*.

- Depending on local custom and circumstances, the closing hymn may be omitted. The hymn selected for the closing hymn may be sung as the final hymn during distribution of Holy Communion.

- Additional hymn choices include:

  "A Lamb Goes Uncomplaining Forth" (*LSB* 438)
  "Chief of Sinners Though I Be" (*LSB* 611)
  "Come to Calvary's Holy Mountain" (*LSB* 435)
  "God's Own Child, I Gladly Say It" (*LSB* 594)
  "Hear Us, Father, When We Pray" (*LSB* 773)
  "In Adam We Have All Been One" (*LSB* 569)
  "In the Very Midst of Life" (*LSB* 755)
  "Jesus Christ, My Sure Defense" (*LSB* 741)
  "Jesus Christ, Our Blessed Savior" (*LSB* 627)
  "Jesus, Refuge of the Weary" (*LSB* 423)
  "Jesus Sinners Doth Receive" (*LSB* 609)
  "Lord Jesus Christ, Life-Giving Bread" (*LSB* 625)
  "Lord, to You I Make Confession" (*LSB* 608)
  "Now Rest beneath Night's Shadow" (*LSB* 880)
  "O Love, How Deep" (*LSB* 544)
  "Savior, When in Dust to Thee" (*LSB* 419)
  "Soul, Adorn Yourself with Gladness" (*LSB* 636)
  "Stricken, Smitten, and Afflicted" (*LSB* 451)
  "Thy Works, Not Mine, O Christ" (*LSB* 565)
  "To Thee, Omniscient Lord of All" (*LSB* 613)

MIDWEEK DIVINE SERVICE

(For use each week. See specific elements on pp. 121–36.)

HYMN OF INVOCATION

Stand

INVOCATION

OPENING ADDRESS

VERSICLES

Kneel/Stand

CONFESSION AND DECLARATION OF GRACE

Stand

INTROIT

KYRIE

SALUTATION AND COLLECT OF THE DAY

Sit

OLD TESTAMENT

PSALM OR GRADUAL

EPISTLE

Stand

VERSE

HOLY GOSPEL

CREED

Sit

HYMN OF THE DAY

SERMON

OFFERING

OFFERTORY

Stand

PRAYER OF THE CHURCH

PREFACE

PROPER PREFACE

SANCTUS

LORD'S PRAYER

THE WORDS OF OUR LORD

PAX DOMINI

Agnus Dei

Sit

Distribution Hymn(s)
(Appropriate hymns and/or choral music may be sung.)

Stand

Nunc Dimittis

Thanksgiving

Post-Communion Collect

Salutation and Benedicamus

Benediction

[Hymn]

Notes on the Midweek Divine Service for the Worship Planner

- This service follows Divine Service, Setting Three in *Lutheran Service Book*.

- Depending on local custom and circumstances, the Hymn of Invocation and/or the closing hymn may be omitted.

- To emphasize the penitential nature of the season of Lent, the use of the Declaration of Grace (the right-hand column in *Lutheran Service Book*) is suggested.

- Use the Collect of the Day for Ash Wednesday.

- The Creed may be omitted or, for the simplicity of the service, the Apostles' Creed may be used.

- The Offering may be received in silence while the altar is prepared for Holy Communion.

- The Offertory ("Create in me") may be sung as the Offering is presented at the altar, or it may precede the Offering, immediately following the Sermon.

MIDWEEK VESPERS

(For use each week. See specific elements on pp. 121–36.)

Stand

OPENING VERSICLES

PSALM

Sit

OFFICE HYMN

READINGS FROM HOLY SCRIPTURE

RESPONSORY FOR LENT

HYMN

SERMON

OFFERING

Stand

CANTICLE

Kneel/Stand

KYRIE

LORD'S PRAYER

COLLECT OF THE DAY

ADDITIONAL COLLECT(S)

COLLECT FOR PEACE

Stand

BENEDICAMUS

BENEDICTION

HYMN

Notes on the Midweek Vespers Service for the Worship Planner

- This service follows the Order of Vespers in *Lutheran Service Book*.

- For the opening Versicles, use the Acclamation for Lent.

- The Offering may be received immediately following the Sermon (as suggested here) or after the Canticle (as suggested in *Lutheran Service Book*). Another option would be to receive it at the entrance to the church as the people arrive or depart.

- The Magnificat (preceded by the Verse) is the suggested Canticle.

- Use the Collect of the Day for Ash Wednesday.

- Depending on local custom and circumstances, the closing hymn may be omitted.

PROPERS FOR MIDWEEK LENTEN SERVICES

The following propers have been selected in support of the Lenten focus on the hymn "O Sacred Head, Now Wounded" (*LSB* 450), thus they focus on the wounds that Christ suffered for the healing of His people. Consideration has been given to the traditional emphases of Lent, as well as to the particular emphases established each week by the Sundays in Lent.

At various points, options have been offered; pastoral discernment will determine what is best suited for the care and catechesis of the congregation.

MIDWEEK 2: THE WOUND OF BETRAYAL

VESPERS

Psalmody: Psalm 4 (antiphon, Psalm 4:3) and/or Psalm 55:2–5 (6–7), 12–18, 22–23 (antiphon, Psalm 55:1) (Note that Psalm 55 is not in the pew edition of *Lutheran Service Book*.)

Office Hymn: "O Christ, Who Art the Light and Day" (*LSB* 882)

Readings: 2 Samuel 15:1–6 (7–12); Revelation 2:1–7 (8–11); Matthew 26:20–25 (or Part I of the Passion Narrative, pp. 487–89 of *Lutheran Service Book: Altar Book*)

Hymn: "O Sacred Head, Now Wounded" (*LSB* 450, selected stanzas)

Collect: It is appropriate to use the Ash Wednesday Collect (*Lutheran Service Book: Altar Book*, 674) as the principal collect at all midweek services during Lent.

Almighty and everlasting God, You despise nothing You have made and forgive the sins of all who are penitent. Create in us new and contrite hearts that, lamenting our sins and acknowledging our wretchedness, we may receive from You full pardon and forgiveness; through Jesus Christ, Your Son, our Lord, who lives and reigns with You and the Holy Spirit, one God, now and forever.

Additional Collect (adapted from *The Lutheran Liturgy*, 345)

Almighty God, our heavenly Father, we give You most humble and hearty thanks that You have given Your only-begotten Son to bear our sins and to make atonement for us on the cross. We pray that, by Your grace, You would grant us to put our whole trust in His redemption, that our faith in You would be strengthened and our souls comforted, and that we be enabled to resist all the assaults of sin. Protect us against the devices of the evil one. In all temptations keep us by Your Holy Spirit and help us to walk according to Your Word, that, being guarded and defended by Your mighty power, we may never depart from Your ways but in the end be saved by Your grace; through Jesus Christ, our Lord.

Closing Hymn: "Abide, O Dearest Jesus" (*LSB* 919)
Additional Hymn Suggestions:
>"A Mighty Fortress Is Our God" (*LSB* 656)
>"Chief of Sinners Though I Be" (*LSB* 611)
>"Come to Calvary's Holy Mountain" (*LSB* 435)
>"From God Can Nothing Move Me" (*LSB* 713)
>"I Walk in Danger All the Way" (*LSB* 716)
>"Jesus, Grant That Balm and Healing" (*LSB* 421)
>"Lord, Keep Us Steadfast in Your Word" (*LSB* 655)
>"Lord of Our Life" (*LSB* 659)
>"O God, My Faithful God" (*LSB* 696)
>"O Love, How Deep" (*LSB* 544)
>"Rise, My Soul, to Watch and Pray" (*LSB* 663)
>"Stricken, Smitten, and Afflicted" (*LSB* 451)
>"The Tree of Life" (*LSB* 561)
>"Triune God, Be Thou Our Stay" (*LSB* 505)

DIVINE SERVICE

Hymn of Invocation: "O Sacred Head, Now Wounded" (*LSB* 450, selected stanzas)

Introit: Psalm 41:5–9 (antiphon, Psalm 41:4)

Collect: It is appropriate to use the Ash Wednesday Collect (*Lutheran Service Book: Altar Book*, 674) as the principle collect at all midweek services during Lent.

Almighty and everlasting God, You despise nothing You have made and forgive the sins of all who are penitent. Create in us new and contrite hearts that, lamenting our sins and acknowledging our wretchedness, we may receive from You full pardon and forgiveness; through Jesus Christ, Your Son, our Lord, who lives and reigns with You and the Holy Spirit, one God, now and forever.

Old Testament: 2 Samuel 15:1–6 (7–12)
Gradual: Psalm 3 (morning) or Psalm 4 (evening)
Epistle: Revelation 2:1–7 (8–11)
Verse: Psalm 55:22
Holy Gospel: Matthew 26:20–25 (or Part I of the Passion Narrative, pp. 487–89 of *Lutheran Service Book: Altar Book*)
Hymn of the Day: "A Lamb Goes Uncomplaining Forth" (*LSB* 438)
Prayer of the Church (adapted from *The Lutheran Liturgy*, 318–19)

O God of our salvation, out of love You sent Your only-begotten Son into the world, that whoever believes in Him should not perish but have everlasting life. Grant us the aid of Your Holy Spirit that we may be firmly assured of this mystery of grace and, cleaving to it always with true faith, may be enabled to cleanse ourselves from all filthiness of the flesh and spirit, and to follow after holiness in the fear of God.

Forgetting those things that are behind and reaching for those things that are to come, may we press toward the mark for the prize of Your high calling in Christ Jesus. So order the course of Your providence toward us that all things may work together for our good. Enable us, through the aid of Your Spirit, so to use the means of salvation we enjoy in the Church that we may be delivered from the power of our sins and be strengthened with all might in the inner man unto every good work.

Make us equal to all duties and trials. Help us to overcome the world. Subdue Satan under our feet. Attend and support us in all our coming in and going out, and lead us by Your hand in the way we ought to walk, that we not come short of Your glory and that no one take from us our crown. And finally, when we have thus endured to the end through Your grace, O most merciful Father, grant that we may die in peace and so enter the everlasting kingdom of our Lord and Savior, Jesus Christ, who lives and reigns with You and the Holy Spirit, one God, now and forever.

Proper Preface: *Lutheran Service Book: Altar Book*, 230 (Lent), 243 (Common III), or 244 (Weekday)

Distribution Hymns: "I Walk in Danger All the Way" (*LSB* 716); "O God, My Faithful God" (*LSB* 696); "Rise, My Soul, to Watch and Pray" (*LSB* 663)

Closing Hymn: "Abide, O Dearest Jesus" (*LSB* 919)

Additional Hymn Suggestions:

"A Mighty Fortress Is Our God" (*LSB* 656)

"Chief of Sinners Though I Be" (*LSB* 611)

"Christ, the Lord of Hosts, Unshaken" (*LSB* 521)

"Come to Calvary's Holy Mountain" (*LSB* 435)

"From God Can Nothing Move Me" (*LSB* 713)

"How Wide the Love of Christ" (*LSB* 535)

"In God, My Faithful God" (*LSB* 745)

"Jesus, Grant That Balm and Healing" (*LSB* 421)

"Jesus, Lead Thou On" (*LSB* 718)

"Lord, Keep Us Steadfast in Your Word" (*LSB* 655)

"Lord of All Nations, Grant Me Grace" (*LSB* 844)

"Lord of Our Life" (*LSB* 659)

"O Love, How Deep" (*LSB* 544)

"Stricken, Smitten, and Afflicted" (*LSB* 451)

"The Tree of Life" (*LSB* 561)

"Through Jesus' Blood and Merit" (*LSB* 746)

"Triune God, Be Thou Our Stay" (*LSB* 505)

MIDWEEK 3: THE WOUND OF APATHY

VESPERS

Psalmody: Psalm 30 (antiphon, Psalm 30:10) and/or Psalm 69:2–15 (antiphon, Psalm 69:1) (Note that Psalm 69 is not in the pew edition of *Lutheran Service Book*.)

Office Hymn: "Christ, Mighty Savior" (*LSB* 881) or "I Lie, O Lord, within Your Care" (*LSB* 885)

Readings: 1 Kings 19:1–8 (9–18); 1 Peter 5:1–11 (or Revelation 3:[7–13] 14–22); Matthew 26:(31–35) 36–46 (or Part II of the Passion Narrative, pp. 490–92 of *Lutheran Service Book: Altar Book*)

Hymn: "O Sacred Head, Now Wounded" (*LSB* 450, selected stanzas)

Additional Collect (adapted from *The Lutheran Liturgy*, 316)

Almighty and everlasting God, our Father in heaven, from You comes every good and perfect gift, and so do we present ourselves before You in the name of Your dear Son, Jesus Christ, with a deep sense of our unworthiness and guilt but also with boldness and confidence in Your infinite mercy. Grant us the remission of all our sins, and make us to know the blessedness of those to whom You do not impute iniquity. Create in us a clean heart, and renew a right spirit within us. Impart to us the power of that faith which overcomes the world, the flesh, and the devil. Fill our hearts with love for You and charity toward all our neighbors in the world. Establish in us the hope of everlasting glory. Strengthen us by Your Spirit to every good work, and make us to grow daily in the grace and knowledge of our Lord Jesus Christ, in whose dear name we pray.

Closing Hymn: "Evening and Morning" (*LSB* 726)
Additional Hymn Suggestions:
     "Chief of Sinners Though I Be" (*LSB* 611)
     "Christ, the Life of All the Living" (*LSB* 420)
     "Hear Us, Father, When We Pray" (*LSB* 773)
     "Hope of the World" (*LSB* 690)
     "I Trust, O Lord, Your Holy Name" (*LSB* 734)
     "Jesus, I Will Ponder Now" (*LSB* 440)
     "Jesus, Refuge of the Weary" (*LSB* 423)
     "Let Us Ever Walk with Jesus" (*LSB* 685)
     "Lord, Thee I Love with All My Heart" (*LSB* 708)
     "My Song Is Love Unknown" (*LSB* 430)
     "O Holy Spirit, Grant Us Grace" (*LSB* 693)
     "Rejoice, My Heart, Be Glad and Sing" (*LSB* 737)
     "Rise! To Arms! With Prayer Employ You" (*LSB* 668)
     "Stricken, Smitten, and Afflicted" (*LSB* 451)
     "Upon the Cross Extended" (*LSB* 453)
     "Wake, Awake, for Night Is Flying" (*LSB* 516)

DIVINE SERVICE

Hymn of Invocation: "Evening and Morning" (*LSB* 726)
Introit: Psalm 30:6–9 (antiphon, Psalm 30:10)
Old Testament: 1 Kings 19:1–8 (9–18)
Gradual: Psalm 54:1–3 (4–6)
Epistle: 1 Peter 5:1–11 (or Revelation 3:[7–13] 14–22)

Verse: Psalm 130:5–6a

Holy Gospel: Matthew 26:(31–35) 36–46 (or Part II of the Passion Narrative, pp. 490–92 of *Lutheran Service Book: Altar Book*)

Hymn of the Day: "O Sacred Head, Now Wounded" (*LSB* 450, selected stanzas)

Prayer of the Church (adapted from *The Lutheran Liturgy*, 320–21, 318)

O Lord, You have been our dwelling place in all generations. Before the mountains were brought forth or You had created the heavens and the earth, even from everlasting to everlasting, You are God. You turn man to destruction and say, "Return, you children of men." For a thousand years in Your sight are but as yesterday when it is past and as a watch in the night. The days of our life are but seventy years, and if by reason of strength they be eighty years, yet their strength is full of labor and sorrow; for it is soon cut off, and we fly away. Enter not into judgment with us, O God, and deliver us not into the bitter pains of eternal death.

O most merciful Savior, forgive our innumerable sins and shortcomings. So impress us with the constant thought of the vanity of the world, the certainty of death, and the judgment to come that we may mortify more and more the lust of the flesh, the lust of the eyes, and the pride of life, and be prepared at all times for the coming of the Son of Man. Keep us mindful that we are strangers and pilgrims on earth, and give us grace to look for the city above, following those who have overcome the world and inherited the promises through faith and trust in You. Help us to work out our own salvation with fear and trembling, that we may die in the peace of Christ, who shall change our vile bodies and fashion them like His own glorious body.

O Lord God, lover of mankind, we most earnestly beseech You to bless all Your people, the flocks of Your fold. Shed abroad the peace of heaven into our hearts, and grant us also the peace of this life. Enliven us with Your loving-kindness, that we may keep and hold fast the testimony of Your mouth and not continue in sin. Deliver all who are in trouble, for You alone are God. In mercy pardon those who have erred, and bring them back from their wanderings.

Impart the consolation of Your heavenly grace to all the sons and daughters of affliction and sorrow. Enable us to finish our course in faith and so make us worthy partakers of the inheritance of all Your saints in light; through Jesus Christ, Your Son, our Lord, who lives and reigns with You and the Holy Spirit, one God, now and forever.

Distribution Hymns: "Jesus, I Will Ponder Now" (*LSB* 440); "Jesus, Grant That Balm and Healing" (*LSB* 421); "Christ, the Life of All the Living" (*LSB* 420)

Closing Hymn: "Jesus, Refuge of the Weary" (*LSB* 423)

Additional Hymn Suggestions:

"Chief of Sinners Though I Be" (*LSB* 611)

"Christ, the Lord of Hosts, Unshaken" (*LSB* 521)

"Go to Dark Gethsemane" (*LSB* 436)

"Hear Us, Father, When We Pray" (*LSB* 773)

"Hope of the World" (*LSB* 690)

"I Trust, O Lord, Your Holy Name" (*LSB* 734)

"Jesus, Thy Blood and Righteousness" (*LSB* 563)

"Let Us Ever Walk with Jesus" (*LSB* 685)

"Lord, Thee I Love with All My Heart" (*LSB* 708)

"My Song Is Love Unknown" (*LSB* 430)

"O Holy Spirit, Grant Us Grace" (*LSB* 693)

"Rejoice, My Heart, Be Glad and Sing" (*LSB* 737)

"Rise! To Arms! With Prayer Employ You" (*LSB* 668)

"Stricken, Smitten, and Afflicted" (*LSB* 451)

"Take My Life and Let It Be" (*LSB* 783)

"Upon the Cross Extended" (*LSB* 453)

"Wake, Awake, for Night Is Flying" (*LSB* 516)

Midweek 4: The Wound of Denial

Vespers

Psalmody: Psalm 147:2–11 (antiphon, Psalm 147:1)

Office Hymn: "All Praise to Thee, My God, This Night" (*LSB* 883)

Readings: Jeremiah 17:5–18 (or Jeremiah 26:[1–7] 8–16); 1 Peter 4:12–19; Matthew 26:(57–68) 69–75 (or Part III of the Passion Narrative, pp. 492–93 of *Lutheran Service Book: Altar Book*)

Hymn: "O Sacred Head, Now Wounded" (*LSB* 450, selected stanzas)

Additional Collect (adapted from *The Lutheran Liturgy*, 317)

O God of Sabaoth, Creator and Preserver of all things, in Your infinite mercy You have given Your only-begotten Son to redeem the children of men, that by His innocent death on the cross He should blot out the handwriting of our sins and reconcile the world to You. For His sake, accept our humble praise and graciously hear our supplications. Give us true repentance; forgive us our sins, negligence, and ignorance; and by Your Holy Spirit grant that we may live according to Your Word. Enable us to cast off the works of darkness, which war against the soul, and deliver us from all our enemies, both visible and invisible, which seek to destroy us. Help us to walk by faith in Your sight, to crucify the flesh, and to keep ourselves pure from all unholy thoughts, words, and actions. Incline our hearts to fear, love, and trust in You above all things, and let them be so fixed with steadfast faith in Christ, Your Son, that, being guided by the light of His truth, we may at length obtain the light and joy of heaven, and give all praise and glory to You; through the same Jesus Christ, our Lord.

Closing Hymn: "Stricken, Smitten, and Afflicted" (*LSB* 451)
Additional Hymn Suggestions:
    "A Lamb Goes Uncomplaining Forth" (*LSB* 438)
    "Come to Calvary's Holy Mountain" (*LSB* 435)
    "From God Can Nothing Move Me" (*LSB* 713)
    "How Clear Is Our Vocation, Lord" (*LSB* 853)
    "I Know My Faith Is Founded" (*LSB* 587)
    "I Walk in Danger All the Way" (*LSB* 716)
    "If Your Beloved Son, O God" (*LSB* 568)
    "In the Cross of Christ I Glory" (*LSB* 427)
    "Jesus, Grant That Balm and Healing" (*LSB* 421)
    "Lord, Help Us Ever to Retain" (*LSB* 865)
    "May God Bestow on Us His Grace" (*LSB* 823)
    "We Sing the Praise of Him Who Died" (*LSB* 429)

DIVINE SERVICE

Hymn of Invocation: "O Sacred Head, Now Wounded" (*LSB* 450, selected stanzas)
    Introit: Psalm 147:5–6, 10–11 (antiphon, Psalm 147:1)
    Old Testament: Jeremiah 17:5–18 (or Jeremiah 26:[1–7] 8–16)
    Gradual: Psalm 147:2–3

Epistle: 1 Peter 4:12–19
Verse: Proverbs 9:10
Holy Gospel: Matthew 26:(57–68) 69–75 (or Part III of the Passion Narrative, pp. 492–93 of *Lutheran Service Book: Altar Book*)
Hymn of the Day: "If Your Beloved Son, O God" (*LSB* 568)
Prayer of the Church (adapted from *The Lutheran Liturgy*, 319–20, 293)

O Almighty God and Father of our Lord Jesus Christ, You are the Holy One and justly offended with us, but You are yet our gracious Lord and merciful Father in Christ Jesus. Be pleased to blot out our sins from Your remembrance, and heal our wounds, that we may sin no more against You. Open our eyes, that we may see and amend our infirmities and follies, and give us a perfect understanding in the way of godliness, that we may walk in it all the days of our pilgrimage. Give us a spirit diligent in the works of our calling, cheerful and zealous in doing Your will, fervent and frequent in prayer, charitable and useful in our dealings. Give us a chaste and healthy body, a pure and holy soul, a sanctified and humble spirit, and preserve our body, soul, and spirit blameless to the coming of our Lord Jesus Christ.

Blessed be Your name, O God of all mercies! You have preserved us again and again from sickness and sorrow, from adverse happenings and a violent death, from the malice of Satan and the evil consequences of our sins. The outgoings of the morning and evening shall praise You, and Your servants shall rejoice in giving You glory and thanks for all Your wonderful dealings with all the children of men and, especially, the members of Your Church.

O Lord, You are the Great Physician of soul and body. You chasten, and You heal. We beseech You mercifully to regard Your servants who are sick or suffering in any way, including especially those of our own household of faith . . . We pray that You would spare their lives and restore their strength. As You have given Your own dear Son to bear our infirmities and sickness, deal compassionately with Your servants, and visit them with Your virtue and power. Into Your hands we commit them; to Your gracious mercy and protection we commend them as to a faithful and merciful God.

Let Your providence and care attend us day and night, that we may never sin against You by idleness or folly, by evil company or private sins, by word or deed, by thought or desire. Conduct us through life by Your Word and Spirit that, when the days of our sojourning on earth are done and the shadow is departed, we may die in Your fear and favor; through Jesus Christ, Your Son, our Lord, who lives and reigns with You and the Holy Spirit, one God, now and forever.

Distribution Hymns: "Stricken, Smitten, and Afflicted" (*LSB* 451); "I Know My Faith Is Founded" (*LSB* 587); "From God Can Nothing Move Me" (*LSB* 713)

Closing Hymn: "May God Bestow on Us His Grace" (*LSB* 823)

Additional Hymn Suggestions:

"A Lamb Goes Uncomplaining Forth" (*LSB* 438)

"Built on the Rock" (*LSB* 645)

"Chief of Sinners Though I Be" (*LSB* 611)

"Christ, the Lord of Hosts, Unshaken" (*LSB* 521)

"Come to Calvary's Holy Mountain" (*LSB* 435)

"How Clear Is Our Vocation, Lord" (*LSB* 853)

"How Sweet the Name of Jesus Sounds" (*LSB* 524)

"I Walk in Danger All the Way" (*LSB* 716)

"In the Cross of Christ I Glory" (*LSB* 427)

"Jesus, Grant That Balm and Healing" (*LSB* 421)

"Jesus, Refuge of the Weary" (*LSB* 423)

"Lord, Help Us Ever to Retain" (*LSB* 865)

"Lord of All Nations, Grant Me Grace" (*LSB* 844)

"We Sing the Praise of Him Who Died" (*LSB* 429)

MIDWEEK 5: THE WOUND OF MOCKERY

VESPERS

Psalmody: Psalm 31:9–20 (21–24) (antiphon, Psalm 31:1) or "Song of Hannah" (*LSB* 928)

Office Hymn: "O Blessed Light, O Trinity" (*LSB* 890) or "Now Rest beneath Night's Shadow" (*LSB* 880)

Readings: Jeremiah 20:7–13 (14–18); 1 Peter 2:(13–17) 18–25; Matthew 27:(11–14) 24–31 (or Part IV of the Passion Narrative, pp. 494–97 in *Lutheran Service Book: Altar Book*)

Hymn: "O Sacred Head, Now Wounded" (*LSB* 450, selected stanzas)

Additional Collect (adapted from *The Lutheran Liturgy*, 318)

O Lord God, in Your steadfast love for all mankind, we most earnestly beseech You to bless Your people, the flocks of Your fold. Shed abroad the peace of heaven in our hearts, and grant us also the peace of this life. Enliven us with Your loving-kindness, so that we may keep and hold fast the testimony of Your mouth and not continue in sin. Deliver all who are in trouble, for You alone are God. In Your mercy, pardon those who have erred, and bring them back from their wanderings. Impart the consolations of Your heavenly grace to all the sons and daughters of affliction and sorrow. Enable us to finish our course in faith, and so make us worthy partakers of the inheritance of all Your saints in light; through Jesus Christ, our Lord.

Closing Hymn: "Hail, Thou Once Despised Jesus" (*LSB* 531) or "A Lamb Goes Uncomplaining Forth" (*LSB* 438)
Additional Hymn Suggestions:
> "By Grace I'm Saved" (*LSB* 566)
> "Christ, the Life of All the Living" (*LSB* 420)
> "God Loved the World So That He Gave" (*LSB* 571)
> "Hear Us, Father, When We Pray" (*LSB* 773)
> "Hope of the World" (*LSB* 690)
> "How Sweet the Name of Jesus Sounds" (*LSB* 524)
> "I Walk in Danger All the Way" (*LSB* 716)
> "In God, My Faithful God" (*LSB* 745)
> "Jesus, I Will Ponder Now" (*LSB* 440)
> "Jesus, Priceless Treasure" (*LSB* 743)
> "O Dearest Jesus, What Law Hast Thou Broken" (*LSB* 439)
> "On My Heart Imprint Your Image" (*LSB* 422)
> "Stricken, Smitten, and Afflicted" (*LSB* 451)
> "The Gospel Shows the Father's Grace" (*LSB* 580)
> "Why Should Cross and Trial Grieve Me" (*LSB* 756)

Divine Service

Hymn of Invocation: "A Lamb Goes Uncomplaining Forth" (*LSB* 438)
Introit: Psalm 2:2–3, 5–6, 10, 12 (antiphon, Psalm 2:11) or "Song of Hannah" (*LSB* 928)
Old Testament: Jeremiah 20:7–13 (14–18)
Gradual: Psalm 31:9–14 (15–18) or "Song of Hannah" (*LSB* 928)
Epistle: 1 Peter 2:(13–17) 18–25

Verse: Psalm 30:1

Holy Gospel: Matthew 27:(11–14) 24–31 (or Part IV of the Passion Narrative, pp. 494–97 in *Lutheran Service Book: Altar Book*)

Hymn of the Day: "Why Should Cross and Trial Grieve Me" (*LSB* 756)

Prayer of the Church (adapted from *The Lutheran Liturgy*, 347)

O Lord Jesus Christ, Lamb of God, You were led forth to the ignominious death of the cross for our sins and numbered with the transgressors, being made a curse for us to satisfy the eternal and immutable justice of God. For this great mercy we give You most hearty praise, honor, and glory, and we pray that You would strengthen our faith and trust in You, that, being redeemed from the curse of the Law, we may be comforted in every temptation with Your all-sufficient merit. Let the preaching of the cross be to us the power and wisdom of God, that by the faithful use of Your Word we may obtain the blessings which You have promised.

Grant us, by Your grace, that our old man may daily be crucified with all our sinful lusts and desires, and that we may henceforth serve not sin, but walk in newness of life. May we also with true faith and sincere devotion follow Your example of meekness in affliction and sorrow, love our enemies, and willingly suffer injury and injustice for Your name's sake.

Draw us to Yourself, as You have come to seek and to save the lost, even as You call all people to Yourself by the word of Your cross. Intercede for us with the Father, even as You prayed for those who reviled and crucified You. And grant that we may continue blameless in steadfast faith and in patient hope to the end. Remember us in Your kingdom, let Your cross be our solace in our final distress, and receive our souls into Your hands; for You have redeemed us, O Lord of truth, and You are the only true and living God, with the Father and the Holy Spirit, now and forever.

Distribution Hymns: "O Sacred Head, Now Wounded" (*LSB* 450); "Jesus, Priceless Treasure" (*LSB* 743); "O Dearest Jesus, What Law Hast Thou Broken" (*LSB* 439)

Closing Hymn: "Hail, Thou Once Despised Jesus" (*LSB* 531)

Additional Hymn Suggestions:
"By Grace I'm Saved" (*LSB* 566)
"Christ, the Life of All the Living" (*LSB* 420)
"Dear Christians, One and All, Rejoice" (*LSB* 556)
"God Loved the World So That He Gave" (*LSB* 571)
"Hear Us, Father, When We Pray" (*LSB* 773)
"Hope of the World" (*LSB* 690)
"How Sweet the Name of Jesus Sounds" (*LSB* 524)
"I Walk in Danger All the Way" (*LSB* 716)
"In God, My Faithful God" (*LSB* 745)
"Jesus, I Will Ponder Now" (*LSB* 440)
"My Faith Looks Up to Thee" (*LSB* 702)
"On My Heart Imprint Your Image" (*LSB* 422)
"Stricken, Smitten, and Afflicted" (*LSB* 451)
"The Gospel Shows the Father's Grace" (*LSB* 580)

MIDWEEK 6: THE WOUND OF ABANDONMENT

VESPERS

Psalmody: Psalm 85 (antiphon, Psalm 85:4) and/or Psalm 22:1–11, 19–24 (antiphon, Psalm 22:27)

Office Hymn: "Abide with Me" (*LSB* 878)

Readings: Jeremiah 30:10–17 (18–21) 22–24; Hebrews 11:32–12:3; Matthew 27:(35–44) 45–50 (or Part V of the Passion Narrative, pp. 497–500 in *Lutheran Service Book: Altar Book*)

Hymn: "O Sacred Head, Now Wounded" (*LSB* 450, selected stanzas)

Additional Collect (adapted from *The Lutheran Liturgy*, 344–45)

O Lord Jesus Christ, we adore Your love and praise Your compassion. We bless You for Your bonds and stripes, for Your crown of thorns and painful cross, for Your bitter agony and death. We bless You that, though You knew no sin, You were made sin for us, that we might be made the righteousness of God in You. May the contemplation of Your holy Passion give us an abiding sense of our own unworthiness and of Your surpassing grace, that, being distressed by our sin, we may be comforted by Your merit. O Christ, the Lamb of God, You take away the sin of the world; do not forsake us in adversity and distress and in the hour of death, but have mercy on us and grant us Your peace. As You have loved us, even so may we, withdrawing our affections from the world and the things that are in the world, love You alone. And as You have left us an example, enable us to follow in Your steps. Grant that, looking to You, the Author and Perfecter of our faith, we may run with patience the race that is set before us and hereafter obtain the end of our faith, even the salvation of our souls; for You live and reign, with the Father and the Holy Spirit, one God, now and forever.

Closing Hymn: "Lord Jesus Christ, with Us Abide" (*LSB* 585) or "O God, Our Help in Ages Past" (*LSB* 733)

Additional Hymn Suggestions:
"A Lamb Goes Uncomplaining Forth" (*LSB* 438)
"Christ, the Life of All the Living" (*LSB* 420)
"From God Can Nothing Move Me" (*LSB* 713)
"God's Own Child, I Gladly Say It" (*LSB* 594)
"Hear Us, Father, When We Pray" (*LSB* 773)
"In the Cross of Christ I Glory" (*LSB* 427)
"Jesus, I Will Ponder Now" (*LSB* 440)
"Jesus, Refuge of the Weary" (*LSB* 423)
"Jesus, Thy Boundless Love to Me" (*LSB* 683)
"Lord Jesus Christ, the Church's Head" (*LSB* 647)
"Stricken, Smitten, and Afflicted" (*LSB* 451)
"Upon the Cross Extended" (*LSB* 453)
"Who Trusts in God a Strong Abode" (*LSB* 714)
"Why Should Cross and Trial Grieve Me" (*LSB* 756)

DIVINE SERVICE

Hymn of Invocation: "Lord Jesus Christ, Be Present Now" (*LSB* 902)

Introit: Psalm 85:2–3, 6–9 (antiphon, Psalm 85:4)

Old Testament: Jeremiah 30:10–17 (18–21) 22–24

Gradual: Psalm 69:16–21

Epistle: Hebrews 11:32–12:3

Verse: Psalm 22:22

Holy Gospel: Matthew 27:(35–44) 45–50 (or Part V of the Passion Narrative, pp. 497–500 in *Lutheran Service Book: Altar Book*)

Hymn of the Day: "O Sacred Head, Now Wounded" (*LSB* 450, selected stanzas)

Prayer of the Church (adapted from *The Lutheran Liturgy*, 342–43)

O Lord Jesus Christ, You are the Author and Perfecter of our faith, who for the joy that was set before You endured the cross, despising the shame. We thank You for Your unspeakable love, in that You have not only procured for us rest by Your sorrow and life by Your death but are also pleased to impart Your saving health to us by the preaching of the cross, the Word of truth.

As You have brought us to this holy season, in which we meditate on the solemn mysteries of Your holy Passion, we beseech You, by Your Holy Spirit enlighten our understanding and direct our will, that we may hear the story of Your sufferings and death with our minds disengaged from all worldly distractions and bent solely on contemplating in devout reverence and for our own salvation the wonders of Your love, into which even the angels desire to look. Enable us to realize both the enormity and the bitterness of our sins for which You were wounded, that we may repent of them, and the unfathomable depths of Your grace, which, where sin abounded, does much more abound, that we may be comforted.

Oh, that Your image, O Man of Sorrows, were deeply engraved on our hearts to make them Yours! Give us the obedience of faith, that we may now and ever after be partakers of Your plenteous redemption. Sprinkle us with Your blood, cleanse our souls from sin, strengthen our hearts with the assurance of our adoption, and transform us into Your image by the renewing of our mind. May the infinite fervor of Your love kindle in us steadfast faith in You and fervent love toward You and toward one another, that we may offer up spiritual sacrifices acceptable to God by You. Have mercy on everyone according to his need, add Your blessing to the services of Your Church during this sacred time, be with us throughout our lives, guide us by Your good and gracious Spirit, and grant that we may finally be acceptable in Your sight.

O Lord, in Your ministry on earth You healed many who were sick with frail and diseased bodies. We pray that You would now also look with mercy on Your servants who suffer in any way, including especially those of our own household of faith . . . And as we are all strangers and pilgrims on earth, help us by true faith and a godly life to prepare for the world to come, doing the work You have given us to do while it is day, before the night comes when no one can work. When our last hour shall come, support us by Your power and receive us into Your everlasting kingdom; for You live and reign with the Father and the Holy Spirit, one God, now and forever.

Distribution Hymns: "My Song Is Love Unknown" (*LSB* 430); "If Thou But Trust in God to Guide Thee" (*LSB* 750); "In the Very Midst of Life" (*LSB* 755)

Closing Hymn: "Lord Jesus Christ, with Us Abide" (*LSB* 585)

Additional Hymn Suggestions:

"A Lamb Goes Uncomplaining Forth" (*LSB* 438)
"Christ, the Life of All the Living" (*LSB* 420)
"Crown Him with Many Crowns" (*LSB* 525)
"From God Can Nothing Move Me" (*LSB* 713)
"God's Own Child, I Gladly Say It" (*LSB* 594)
"Hear Us, Father, When We Pray" (*LSB* 773)
"How Wide the Love of Christ" (*LSB* 535)
"In the Cross of Christ I Glory" (*LSB* 427)
"Jesus, I Will Ponder Now" (*LSB* 440)
"Jesus, Refuge of the Weary" (*LSB* 423)
"Jesus, Thy Boundless Love to Me" (*LSB* 683)
"Lord Jesus Christ, the Church's Head" (*LSB* 647)
"Stricken, Smitten, and Afflicted" (*LSB* 451)
"The Royal Banners Forward Go" (*LSB* 455)
"The Son of God Goes Forth to War" (*LSB* 661)
"Upon the Cross Extended" (*LSB* 453)
"We Sing the Praise of Him Who Died" (*LSB* 429)
"Who Trusts in God a Strong Abode" (*LSB* 714)
"Why Should Cross and Trial Grieve Me" (*LSB* 756)

Maundy Thursday
A Meal for the Wounded

Rite of Preparation

The congregation and pastor(s) enter in silence.
Kneel/Stand

The Litany

Collect

Almighty and everlasting God, You despise nothing You have made and forgive the sins of all who are penitent. Create in us new and contrite hearts that, lamenting our sins and acknowledging our wretchedness, we may receive from You full pardon and forgiveness; through Jesus Christ, Your Son, our Lord, who lives and reigns with You and the Holy Spirit, one God, now and forever.
Sit

Hymn: "Baptismal Waters Cover Me" (*LSB* 616)

Kneel/Stand

Service of Corporate Confession and Absolution

Divine Service

Stand

Processional Hymn: "Now, My Tongue, the Mystery Telling" (*LSB* 630)

Introit: Psalm 116:1–4 (antiphon, Psalm 116:5)

Kyrie

Gloria in Excelsis

Salutation and Collect of the Day

Sit

OLD TESTAMENT: Exodus 24:3–11

GRADUAL: Hebrews 9:12a, c, 15a; Psalm 111:9a

EPISTLE: 1 Corinthians 11:23–32

Stand

VERSE: John 13:1b

HOLY GOSPEL: John 13:1–17, 31b–35

NICENE CREED

Sit

HYMN OF THE DAY: "O Lord, We Praise Thee" (*LSB* 617)

SERMON

Stand

OFFERTORY

Sit

OFFERING

Stand

PRAYER OF THE CHURCH

O Lord Jesus Christ, our only Mediator and Redeemer, we thank You that on the night You were handed over to Your voluntary suffering and death, You instituted for us the Holy Sacrament of Your true body and blood as a perpetual memorial of Your atoning sacrifice, a solemn pledge of Your mercy and continual presence, and a salutary means of grace.

You are the true and only Passover Lamb in this Holy Supper, and by giving us Your body to eat and Your blood to drink You grant us a wondrous communion with You as very members of Your Body. Here do You impart and seal to us the merits of Your death, the forgiveness of our sins, so that by these, Your gifts of life and salvation, we are righteous and acceptable in the sight of God.

O Lord, we have in no way deserved Your goodness, nor can we ever sufficiently thank You for Your loving-kindness toward us. We beseech You, however, to strengthen and sustain us by this blessed and holy

138

Sacrament. Enable us, by Your grace, daily to appropriate and experience the blessings of Your Passion in such a way that we may heartily praise You for our redemption and from day to day be more intimately united to You by faith and love.

Kindle in us always such a fervent longing for blessed communion with You in the Holy Supper that we may come often to Your table. By Your Holy Spirit also work in us true repentance and a steadfast faith in Your gracious promises, a sincere desire to be in perfect charity with all people, and the earnest purpose to amend our sinful lives, that we may be worthy recipients of the Holy Sacrament and, with full pardon of all our sins, be enlivened in the way of righteousness, that we may serve You in holiness and pureness of living and give You continual thanks for all Your goodness.

May Your Holy Supper be a source of comfort to the penitent, a means of enrichment to the poor in spirit, to the sick a sweet relief from the bitterness of pain, and to the dying a pledge of their inheritance with the saints in light.

Abide in Your Church with Your gracious presence, and let her at all times be a faithful keeper and dispenser of the heavenly treasures entrusted to her for those who believe in You. Bless the right use of the means of grace wherever the remembrance of Your death is kept, until You come to judge the living and the dead. Let Your Word and Sacrament strengthen our souls during the days of our pilgrimage on earth, until hereafter we partake of Your Supper with You in Your Father's kingdom; for You live and reign with Him and with the Holy Spirit, one God, now and forever.

C: Amen.

Service of the Sacrament

Preface

Proper Preface

Sanctus

Lord's Prayer

The Words of Our Lord

PAX DOMINI

AGNUS DEI

Sit

DISTRIBUTION HYMNS

"O Sacred Head, Now Wounded" (*LSB* 450)
"Lord Jesus Christ, Life-Giving Bread" (*LSB* 625)
"Jesus Christ, Our Blessed Savior" (*LSB* 627)

Stand

POST-COMMUNION COLLECT

STRIPPING OF THE ALTAR

The Communion vessels are reverently removed from the altar, the altar is stripped, and the chancel is cleared in preparation for the solemn services of Good Friday.

When the stripping of the altar is complete, the pastor(s) and congregation leave in silence.

NOTES ON THE MAUNDY THURSDAY SERVICE FOR THE WORSHIP PLANNER

Maundy Thursday marks a transition within Holy Week from Lent to the Holy Triduum. In this it serves as something of a bookend to Ash Wednesday at the beginning of Lent. The historic Gospel for this day (John 13) recounts the washing of the disciples' feet by our Lord. Although this is an example of Christian love for the neighbor, the foot washing is first and foremost a demonstration of the Lord's enduring love for His own and a depiction of our return to the significance of Holy Baptism through contrition and repentance, confession and faith in the forgiveness of sins. The penitential discipline of Lent has brought us to this point, and Christ Jesus, our Savior, loves us to the end. The dust and ashes of sin and death are washed away by Jesus' word of Holy Absolution, and those who have been humbled by the Law are exalted by the One who humbles Himself, even to death, in order to serve us in love with His own holy body and precious blood.

Although Maundy Thursday is a culmination and completion of Lent, it is also the beginning of the Paschal Feast, which remembers with thanksgiving the sacrificial death and great salvation of the Lamb of God. Maundy Thursday is the first of three sacred days that together constitute the Church's celebration of both the cross and the resurrection of the Lord. Jesus Christ is the true Passover Lamb, who is sacrificed for us, whose blood covers us from death, whose body feeds us for life and salvation in the freedom of the Gospel; yet He is the same Lord God who by His mighty, outstretched arms brings us out of slavery, through the water and the wilderness, into the promised land, and He feeds us on the way.

With its rich and varied emphases, there are different ways and means of observing Maundy Thursday. It may be best to consider the day incrementally. Thus the congregation may gather in the morning for The Litany and for Corporate Confession and Absolution, both in culmination of the Lenten fast and in expectation of the evening Feast. If it is unlikely that many members of the congregation will be able to participate in such a morning service, the same opportunity may be provided in the late afternoon or early evening, but still prior to and distinct from the Divine Service.

Prior to sundown, the color of Maundy Thursday is appropriately the scarlet of Passion Sunday (or the violet of Lent). This fits the penitential character of The Litany and of corporate confession.

After sundown, the color of the day at an evening Divine Service is preferably white. For this reason, also, there should be a clear separation of the penitential rites and services from the evening feast. Although Maundy Thursday may be observed with a more penitential emphasis, it rightly bears a festive mood. Although the Gloria Patri and the Alleluia continue to be omitted, traditionally the Gloria in Excelsis is sung on this occasion. Typically, the Maundy Thursday service is marked by restrained exuberance throughout the Divine Service, until the stripping of the altar concludes this portion of the Triduum with a distinct turning toward the solemn depths of Good Friday. Maundy Thursday looks ahead to both the Passion and the resurrection, and so looks to the Lord's cross as the very tree of life from which our Savior feeds us.

- The rites of preparation may be observed in the morning or late afternoon.

- The Litany is from *Lutheran Service Book*.

- The collect in the Rite of Preparation is the Collect of the Day for Ash Wednesday.

- The Service of Corporate Confession and Absolution is found on pages 290–91 of *Lutheran Service Book* (pages 422–24 of *Lutheran Service Book: Altar Book*).

- If the preparation rites are observed separately from the Divine Service, the pastor(s) and congregation leave in silence.

- If the rites of preparation are followed immediately by the Divine Service, a pause is appropriate, and the color of the day should be changed to white before the Divine Service begins.

- This service is based on Setting Three of the Divine Service in *Lutheran Service Book*.

- The Prayer of the Day is adapted from pages 345–47 of *The Lutheran Liturgy*.

- The Offering may be received in silence while the altar is prepared for Holy Communion.

- During the stripping of the altar, Psalm 22 is chanted or spoken. For further details on the stripping of the altar, see pages 506–7 of *Lutheran Service Book: Altar Book*.

- The Benediction is not given until the conclusion of the Triduum at the Easter Vigil.

- Additional hymn choices include:

  "All Christians Who Have Been Baptized" (*LSB* 596)
  "Chief of Sinners Though I Be" (*LSB* 611)
  "Come to Calvary's Holy Mountain" (*LSB* 435)
  "Father Most Holy" (*LSB* 504)
  "Go to Dark Gethsemane" (*LSB* 436)
  "Hear Us, Father, When We Pray" (*LSB* 773)
  "Hope of the World" (*LSB* 690)
  "How Sweet the Name of Jesus Sounds" (*LSB* 524)
  "How Wide the Love of Christ" (*LSB* 535)
  "Jesus Comes Today with Healing" (*LSB* 620)
  "Jesus, Grant That Balm and Healing" (*LSB* 421)
  "Jesus, Refuge of the Weary" (*LSB* 423)
  "Jesus, Thy Boundless Love to Me" (*LSB* 683)
  "Let All Mortal Flesh Keep Silence" (*LSB* 621)
  "Not All the Blood of Beasts" (*LSB* 431)
  "Soul, Adorn Yourself with Gladness" (*LSB* 636)
  "The Death of Jesus Christ, Our Lord" (*LSB* 634)
  "The Gifts Christ Freely Gives" (*LSB* 602)
  "Thee We Adore, O Hidden Savior" (*LSB* 640)
  "Thy Body, Given for Me, O Savior" (*LSB* 619)
  "Thy Works, Not Mine, O Christ" (*LSB* 565)
  "Wide Open Stand the Gates" (*LSB* 639)

Good Friday
THE WOUNDS THAT HEAL

The congregation and pastor(s) enter in silence.
Kneel/Stand

COLLECT OF THE DAY

Sit

OLD TESTAMENT: Isaiah 52:13–53:12

Silence
Kneel/Stand

COLLECT

Sit

EPISTLE: Hebrews 4:14–16; 5:7–9

Silence
Kneel/Stand

COLLECT

Sit

HYMN: "Jesus, I Will Ponder Now" (*LSB* 440)

READING OF THE PASSION

Silence
Sit

SERMON: The Wounds That Heal (Isaiah 53:1–6)

HYMN OF THE DAY:
"A Lamb Goes Uncomplaining Forth" (*LSB* 438)

Kneel/Stand

THE BIDDING PRAYER

A: Let us pray for the whole Christian Church, that our Lord God would undertake to defend it against all the assaults and temptations of the adversary and to keep it perpetually upon the true foundation, Jesus Christ:

P: Almighty and everlasting God, You who have revealed Your glory to all nations in Jesus Christ and the Word of His truth, we beseech You to keep in safety the works of Your mercy so that Your Church, spread throughout all nations, may serve You in true faith and persevere in the confession of Your name; through Jesus Christ, our Lord.

C: Amen.

A: Let us pray for the ministers of the Word, for all estates in the Church, and for all the people of God:

P: Almighty and everlasting God, by whose Spirit the whole body of the Church is governed and sanctified, receive the supplications and prayers which we offer before You for all estates in Your Holy Church, that all members of the same may truly and godly serve You in their vocation and ministry; through Jesus Christ, our Lord.

C: Amen.

A: Let us pray for our catechumens, that our Lord God would open their hearts and the door of His mercy, that, having received the remission of all their sins by the washing of regeneration, they may be mindful of their baptismal covenant and evermore be found in Christ Jesus, our Lord:

P: Almighty and everlasting God, You who always multiplies Your Church, and with Your light and grace strengthens the hearts of those whom You have regenerated, confirming unto them Your covenant and faithfulness, grant unto our catechumens increase both of faith and knowledge that they may rejoice in their Baptism and heartily renew their covenant with You.

C: Amen.

A: Let us pray for all in authority and especially for the government of the United States, that we may lead a quiet and peaceable life in all godliness and honesty:

P: O merciful Father in heaven, You who holds in Your hand all the might of man and who has ordained the powers that be for the punishment of evildoers and for the praise of those who do well, and of whom comes all rule and authority in the kingdoms of the world, we humbly beseech You, graciously regard Your servants, the president of the United States, the governor of this commonwealth, our judges and magistrates, and all the rulers of the earth, that all who receive the sword as Your ministers may bear it according to Your Commandment; through Christ, our Lord.

C: Amen.

A: Let us pray our Lord God Almighty that He would deliver the world from all error, take away disease, ward off famine, open the prisons, set free those in bondage, grant a safe return to the wayfarers, health to the sick, and to our mariners a harbor of safety:

P: Almighty and everlasting God, the consolation of the sorrowful and the strength of the weak, may the prayers of those who in any tribulation or distress cry unto You graciously come before You, so that in all their necessities they may mark and receive Your manifold help and comfort; through Christ, our Lord.

C: Amen.

A: Let us pray for all those who have erred from the way of the truth, or caused schism in the Church, that the Lord our God would deliver them from their error and bring them to the faith and fellowship of His Holy Church:

P: Almighty God, our heavenly Father, whose property it is always to have mercy, we most earnestly beseech You to visit with Your fatherly correction all who have erred and gone astray from the truth of Your Holy Word and to bring them to a due sense of their error that they may again with hearty faith receive and hold fast Your unchangeable truth; through Jesus Christ, Your Son, our Lord.

C: Amen.

A: Let us pray for the unbelievers, that God would take away their sin and deliver them from their false and dumb idols to serve the true and living God and Jesus Christ, His only Son, our Lord:

P: Almighty and everlasting God, You who desires not the death of a sinner but would have all people to repent and live, hear our prayers for those who do not have the true faith, take away iniquity from their hearts, and turn them from their idols unto the living and true God and to Your only Son. Gather them into Your Holy Church, to the glory of Your name; through Jesus Christ, Your Son, our Lord.

C: Amen.

A: Let us pray for peace, that we may come to the knowledge of God's Holy Word and walk before Him as becomes Christians:

P: Almighty and everlasting God, King of glory and Lord of heaven and earth, by whose Spirit all things are governed, by whose providence all things are ordered, who is the God of peace and the Author of all concord, grant us, we beseech You, Your heavenly peace and concord that we may serve You in true fear, to the praise and glory of Your name; through Christ, our Lord.

C: Amen.

A: Let us pray for our enemies, that God would remember them in mercy and graciously grant to them such things as are both needful for them and profitable to their salvation:

P: O almighty, everlasting God, who through Your only Son, our blessed Lord, has commanded us to love our enemies, to do good to those who hate us, and to pray for those who persecute us, we earnestly beseech You that by Your gracious visitation all our enemies may be led to true repentance and may have the same love and be of one accord and of one mind and heart with us and with Your whole Christian Church; through Christ, our Lord.

C: Amen.

A: Let us pray for the fruits of the earth, that God would send down His blessing upon them and graciously dispose our hearts to enjoy them in submission to His holy will:

P: O Lord, Father Almighty, who by Your Word has created and still blesses and upholds all things, we pray You so to reveal unto us Your Word, our Lord Jesus Christ, that, as He dwells in our hearts, we may by Your grace be made worthy to receive Your blessing on all the fruits of the earth and whatsoever pertains to our bodily need; through Christ, our Lord.

C: Amen.

P: Finally, let us pray for all those things for which our Lord would have us ask, saying:

C: Our Father who art in heaven . . .

Stand

Adoration of the Cross

Kneel/Sit

Reproaches

Sit

Hymn: "Sing, My Tongue, the Glorious Battle" (*LSB* 454)

If the Sacrament of the Altar is not administered, the service ends with the Concluding Collect and hymn.

Stand

PREFACE

LORD'S PRAYER

THE WORDS OF OUR LORD

PAX DOMINI

Sit

DISTRIBUTION HYMNS

"O Darkest Woe" (*LSB* 448)
"Jesus, Grant That Balm and Healing" (*LSB* 421)
"The Death of Jesus Christ, Our Lord" (*LSB* 634)
"O Dearest Jesus, What Law Hast Thou Broken" (*LSB* 439)

Stand

CONCLUDING COLLECT

HYMN: "The Royal Banners Forward Go" (*LSB* 455)
The pastor(s) and congregation leave in silence.

NOTES ON THE GOOD FRIDAY SERVICE
FOR THE WORSHIP PLANNER

Good Friday stands at the heart and center of the Triduum even as Christ's death on the cross, which this day commemorates and celebrates, stands at the heart and center of the Christian faith and life. The service of this day is marked by the Church's deepest humility and most solemn reverence, for she gives her attention to the cross and Passion of her dear Lord and Savior, Jesus Christ. Her sorrow and contrition do not give way to despair, however; nor does she mourn the death of Christ. Rather, in repentant faith the Church gives thanks for Christ's atoning sacrifice and lays hold of His redemption in the hearing of His Gospel (and in the eating and drinking of His body and blood).

Although the Chief Service of Good Friday is appropriately held between the hours of 12 noon and 3 p.m., nevertheless it may be held whenever the majority of the congregation will be able to attend.

The rites and ceremonies of the Good Friday service are profound and powerful and invite deliberate care, calm, and an unhurried approach that allows for a quietly eloquent proclamation of the Passion of the Christ. It is easy to overdo the drama of the day and of the service with theatrical effort, but careful study of the notes and rubrics of the service will help to maintain the appropriate focus.

The color of the day is black, though the altar remains bare (other than for the vessels of the Lord's Supper, at that point in the service when the Sacrament of the Altar may be celebrated). For the bulk of the service, the pastor(s) may be vested in cassock and surplice; the preacher may wear a stole (preferably black) for the sermon.

- This service is taken from pages 512–22 of *Lutheran Service Book: Altar Book*.

- The congregation stands for the concluding portions of the Reading of the Passion, beginning with John 19:16b–24 (Jesus' crucifixion), and continues to stand through the final stanza of the hymn.

- As the Church remembers with thanksgiving the suffering and death of her Lord and Savior for the redemption and reconciliation of the world, it is particularly fitting that she should pray and intercede for the entire world in His name. The Bidding Prayer does this most beautifully and profoundly, identifying all sorts of particular conditions and needs. Such prayer is not historically unique to Good Friday, but was typical of the Church's prayer from its earliest days. Because the most solemn occasions also tend to be the most conservative in form and practice, the Bidding Prayer has been retained as part of the venerable character of Good Friday. The Bidding Prayer included here is adapted from that found on pages 274–77 of *The Lutheran Liturgy* and pages 107–12 of Wilhelm Löhe, *Liturgy for Christian Congregations of the Lutheran Faith*, 3d ed., edited by J. Deinzer, translated by F. C. Longaker (1902).

An updated and shorter form of the Bidding Prayer is found on pages 514–17 of *Lutheran Service Book: Altar Book*.

With either form, an assistant minister announces each of the bids from the lectern; the presiding pastor voices each of the petitions. If possible, the congregation may kneel for the Bidding Prayer, and the presiding pastor may kneel before the altar (at or near a rough-hewn cross, if this is part of local custom and practice).

- The rite associated with the adoration of the cross can be found on page 517 of *Lutheran Service Book: Altar Book*. There are two options associated with this rite. If the rough-hewn cross is carried in procession and placed in the chancel at this point in the service, the sentence "Behold, the life-giving cross on which was hung the salvation of the world" and its response are sung or spoken at three points in the procession. If the cross is already in position at or near the altar, the sentence and response are sung three times, pausing after each for adoration of the cross. The cross is not adored as though it were a relic or a magic talisman, but as a sacred sign of the Lord's redemption (similar to standing for the Holy Gospel).

- There are differences of opinion as to whether the Sacrament of the Altar should be celebrated on Good Friday, and no definitive answer may be dictated. The Roman Catholic and Eastern Orthodox faiths distribute Holy Communion on this day from elements consecrated on Maundy Thursday and reserved intentionally for this purpose. Lutherans should be reluctant to follow such a practice, yet they do also recognize the appropriateness and benefits of receiving the body and blood of Christ on this day as the very fruits of His holy cross. A satisfying and salutary way of celebrating the Sacrament of the Altar on Good Friday is suggested on pages 512, 522–24 of *Lutheran Service Book: Altar Book*. The Communion linens, vessels, and elements are brought to the altar and the celebrant is vested in alb (and chasuble) during the hymn "Sing, My Tongue, the Glorious Battle." The Service of the Sacrament is marked by a reverent simplicity, spoken rather than sung. The Sanctus and the Agnus Dei are not sung; however, hymns of the Passion may be sung during the distribution. The Communion vessels and linens are removed from the altar during the singing of the service's concluding hymn.

- The Benediction is not given until the conclusion of the Triduum at the Easter Vigil.

- Additional hymn choices include:

  "Christ, the Lord of Hosts, Unshaken" (*LSB* 521)
  "Stricken, Smitten, and Afflicted" (*LSB* 451)
  "Thy Works, Not Mine, O Christ" (*LSB* 565)
  "Upon the Cross Extended" (*LSB* 453)

EASTER VIGIL

The congregation and pastor(s) gather at a designated place outside of the church.

SERVICE OF LIGHT

EASTER PROCLAMATION (EXSULTET)

Candles held by members of the congregation are extinguished, and the people are seated.

SERVICE OF READINGS

THE CREATION: Genesis 1:1–2:3

THE FLOOD: Genesis 7:1–5, 11–18; 8:6–18; 9:8–13

THE TESTING OF ABRAHAM: Genesis 22:1–18

ISRAEL'S DELIVERANCE AT THE RED SEA: Exodus 14:10–15:1

Stand

CANTICLE: "Song of Moses and Israel" (*LSB* 925)

Sit

A NEW HEART AND A NEW SPIRIT: Ezekiel 36:24–28

THE VALLEY OF DRY BONES: Ezekiel 37:1–14

JOB CONFESSES THE REDEEMER: Job 19:20–27

JONAH PREACHES TO NINEVEH: Jonah 3:1–10

THE FIERY FURNACE: Daniel 3:1–30

Stand

CANTICLE: "All You Works of the Lord" (*LSB* 931)

Service of Holy Baptism

Service of Prayer

Litany of the Resurrection

The congregation may be seated while the altar is prepared for Holy Communion.

Service of the Word

Stand

Easter Acclamation

Hymn of Praise: Gloria in Excelsis

Holy Gospel: Mark 16:1–8

Sit

Homily

Stand

Service of the Sacrament

Preface

Proper Preface

Sanctus

Prayer of Thanksgiving

Lord's Prayer

The Words of Our Lord

Pax Domini

Agnus Dei

DISTRIBUTION HYMNS

"All the Earth with Joy Is Sounding" (*LSB* 462)
"At the Lamb's High Feast We Sing" (*LSB* 633)
"With High Delight Let Us Unite" (*LSB* 483)

POST-COMMUNION COLLECT

BLESSING AND BENEDICTION

CLOSING HYMN:
"Come, You Faithful, Raise the Strain" (*LSB* 487)

Notes on the Easter Vigil for the Worship Planner

The Great Vigil of Easter, kept on the Eve of the Resurrection of Our Lord, is the culmination of the Holy Triduum. It brings to a festive completion the three-day service that began on Maundy Thursday and continued on Good Friday. In itself, the Easter Vigil is a transitional service. In much the same way that Maundy Thursday was both the conclusion of Lent and the beginning of the Triduum, so the Easter Vigil both completes the Triduum and ushers in the Fifty Days of Eastertide. This transition is poignantly manifested in the course of the vigil, which progresses purposefully from darkness to light. It celebrates specifically the passage of Christ from death into life, and the Church's passage through death into life with Him through Holy Baptism. The night begins with hushed anticipation, proceeds with eager expectation, and finally climaxes in the exuberant celebration of the Paschal Feast.

The Easter Vigil is very much a Christian "Passover," that is, a celebration of the great exodus that Christ Jesus, the Lamb of God, accomplished by His sacrificial death and brought to light in His resurrection from the dead. All that the Lord God did for Israel in bringing His people out of Egypt and into the Promised Land He has perfectly fulfilled for all the baptized, who are the new Israel, in His cross and resurrection. In Holy Baptism we have come out of Egypt and have crossed the Red Sea with Him and have entered with Him into Canaan through the Jordan. In the Paschal Feast of Holy Communion, we eat and drink the true Passover Lamb. His blood covers us and protects us from sin, death, and hell; His body feeds and sustains us on our way.

In particular, the Easter Vigil proclaims and confesses that as we have died with Christ by our Baptism into His death, so do we also rise with Him and live with Him in newness of life. It is for us that He died and rose from the dead. The Vigil lays hold of that sure and certain hope in the Gospel, or, better, the Vigil lays hold of us and brings us with Christ out of death into His life. It does so not by any sort of magic, but by the Word and Spirit of God.

Numerous resources are available on the history and significance of the Easter Vigil, and these will be most helpful to those interested in becoming acquainted with this service and introducing it to their congregations. With its rites, ceremonies, and propers, the vigil itself catechizes pastors and their congregations in the paschal mystery celebrated on this night. The most important preparation, therefore, is for service participants to study carefully and rehearse the notes and rubrics of the Easter Vigil (see pp. 529–51 in *Lutheran Service Book: Altar Book*). When all is well prepared and the service can proceed according to its proper rhythm, the Word of God in the readings and prayers of the Easter Vigil will do its own work among the people of God.

Lutheran Service Book: Altar Book lays out the Easter Vigil in six parts: the Service of Light, the Service of Readings, the Service of Holy Baptism, the Service of Prayer, the Service of the Word, and the Service of the Sacrament. Each part has its own integrity and contributes to the progression of the whole. The Service of Light, in which the paschal candle is consecrated for use and lighted as a sign of the Lord's resurrection, may take place at a bonfire outside the church building. To accentuate the continuity of this night with the Passion of our Lord, the gathering may occur where the congregation assembled for the procession with palms on Passion Sunday. After the consecration of the paschal candle, the people follow it into the church, even as Israel followed the pillar of cloud by day and the pillar of fire by night in the exodus from Egypt. During this procession, "The Light of Christ" ("Thanks be to God") is chanted at three points, which may replicate the points at which the sentence "Behold, the life-giving cross" was stated during the adoration of the cross in the Good Friday service. These ceremonial associations contribute to the way in which the Easter Vigil holds together the cross and resurrection of the Lord Jesus Christ as the New Testament Passover.

The Service of Light crescendos in the chanting of the Exsultet (which ideally is sung rather than spoken). This beautiful proclamation of the paschal mystery sets the tone of the entire Easter Vigil, celebrating the fulfillment of the Old Testament exodus in the resurrection of the Christ. It rings out in the night, in much the same way that the candles break into the darkness with their shimmering light. There is the tension of waiting, a pregnant expectation of that which has already been accomplished but has yet to be openly announced. It is no secret that Christ has risen from the dead—no more so now than on Ash Wednesday or at any other time throughout Lent. Yet the Church on earth lives in, with, and under the cross of Christ; thus she experiences the now-and-not-yet of the resurrection in the Word of the Lord.

Although the handheld candles of the congregation should be carefully extinguished at the end of the Exsultet, the Service of Readings should proceed in semidarkness, with only as much light as necessary for the reading of the Holy Scriptures and for the prayers and canticles of the people. The Readings are the distinctive and definitive heart of the Easter Vigil. They set forth a series of Old Testament prophecies and types of the Christ, of His cross and resurrection, and of the Church's participation in His dying and rising again. It is not expected that congregations will employ all twelve Readings, but as many of these as possible should be used. At least the first three Readings should always be used (the creation, the flood, and the exodus), and preferably the twelfth Reading (the three men in the fiery furnace). A selection of nine Readings is given here, along with two canticles. The congregation should sit for the Readings, kneel for the collects that follow each Reading, and stand for the psalms or canticles that may intersperse the Readings. Because the Church waits on the Lord in steadfast faith and hope by giving attention to His Word, there is no need to hurry through the Readings. Congregations comprised largely of younger members may arrange to observe the Easter Vigil through the hours of the night, culminating in the early dawn of Easter Sunday. In such a case (presumably rare), all of the Readings would be used, each followed by its collect, the appropriate psalm or canticle, and separated with periods of silence. The Readings do not require commentary because within the context of the entire week, the collects, psalms, and canticles provide appropriate and sufficient reflection of the Word by which the Lord catechizes His people and accomplishes His purposes among them.

Whether or not there are catechumens to be baptized at the Easter Vigil, the Service of Baptism follows the Readings as a return to the death and resurrection of repentance and faith that all the baptized share with Christ by the washing of water with His Word and Spirit. Here is the crossing of the Red Sea with the One who is greater than Moses, which already anticipates the crossing of the Jordan with the New Testament Joshua (Jesus, the Christ). This returning to the significance of Holy Baptism through contrition, repentance, and faith in the forgiveness of sins is to be the daily and lifelong discipline of every Christian. It is here embraced at the very heart of the Easter Vigil, in remembrance and celebration of the cross and resurrection of Christ. It is not meant to replace the daily taking up of the cross to follow Jesus as His disciples, but it is observed in service and support of that Christian faith and life. This is the fulfillment of Lent and the rebirth of an Easter life.

It is in that newness of life in Christ that the Church proceeds with the Divine Service that throughout the year constitutes her weekly proclamation of His death and celebration of His resurrection. The Divine Service of the Easter Vigil is somewhat simpler than the usual Sunday observance and is not as full and festive as the Chief Divine Service on Easter Sunday will be. The same basic movement takes place: from the Word of the Gospel to the Word made flesh in Holy Communion, received in faith and with thanksgiving. In this case, the Prayer of the

Church (in the Litany of the Resurrection) precedes the basic pattern of the Word preached and the Sacrament administered, which serves to further heighten the unity of the Holy Gospel and Holy Communion.

Indeed, the Service of the Word at the Easter Vigil is really as much or more a part of the entire Eucharistic Rite rather than a separate component. In contrast to the deliberate and steady pacing of the Readings, the Service of the Word proceeds forward swiftly. Ideally, this would occur around midnight, as there is now a striking transition from darkness to light, from the sobriety of Holy Week to the sights and sounds and celebration of the Easter feast. That is signaled by the Easter acclamation: "Alleluia! Christ is risen! He is risen indeed! Alleluia!" The altar candles are now lighted from the paschal candle, the lights in the church are turned on, bells are rung, the organ opens up in jubilation, the Gloria in Excelsis is sung, and the Lord's altar is prepared for the Sacrament (there is no offering or offertory in the usual manner).

The proclamation of the Easter Gospel (Mark 16:1–8) declares the crucified and risen One who appears among His own and gives to them His body and His blood. It is by and with His Gospel Word and Holy Sacrament that Christ abides among the people of this congregation in this time and place. The preaching of this Gospel should be straightforward and direct, brief and to the point. All of Holy Week and the entire Easter Vigil have been an extended proclamation and catechesis of the Word, the Law and the Gospel, to repentant faith in the Lord Jesus Christ. Therefore it is neither necessary nor desirable to have a lengthy sermon at this point. The historic homilies of John Chrysostom or Gregory of Nazianzus are among those that can serve the purpose of this occasion beautifully.

The Service of the Sacrament (Eucharistic Rite) will follow according to one of the usual settings of the Divine Service, beginning with the Preface. Here it is recommended that Setting One or Two be used. Setting Three may surely be preferred in some congregations, but neither Setting Four nor Five should be chosen for use at the Easter Vigil. Note the special Post-Communion Collect appointed for the Easter Vigil (pp. 550–51 in *Lutheran Service Book: Altar Book*).

The color of the day at the Easter Vigil is white and/or gold. However, the church should be kept in semidarkness until the Service of the Word, at which point there is a transition to all the trappings of Easter, as previously indicated. Depending on the circumstances, the altar may be dressed and adorned with the appropriate paraments, Easter flowers, and other accoutrements at this point in the service. The logistics for such a transition require planning and rehearsal to avoid awkwardness or uncertainty. Similarly, the celebrant and his assistant(s) may prefer to be vested in cassock and surplice, but at this point they would vest in alb (and chasuble for the celebrant) for the Service of the Word and Sacrament.

- During the Service of Readings, each reading is followed by the collect appointed in *Lutheran Service Book: Altar Book*. The congregation may kneel for each collect but should be seated for each reading.

- It is suggested that the Gloria in Excelsis (*Lutheran Service Book*, p. 154 or 170) be used as the Hymn of Praise in the Service of the Word. Another option is the newer Hymn of Praise: "This Is the Feast."

- Note the special Post-Communion Collect and blessing appointed for the Easter Vigil (pp. 550–51 in *Lutheran Service Book: Altar Book*).

- Additional hymn choices include:

  "Christ Is Arisen" (*LSB* 459)
  "Christ Jesus Lay in Death's Strong Bands" (*LSB* 458)
  "He Is Arisen! Glorious Word" (*LSB* 488)
  "I Am Content! My Jesus Ever Lives" (*LSB* 468)
  "If Christ Had Not Been Raised from Death" (*LSB* 486)
  "Jesus Lives! The Victory's Won" (*LSB* 490)
  "Now All the Vault of Heaven Resounds" (*LSB* 465)
  "Our Paschal Lamb, That Sets Us Free" (*LSB* 473)
  "The Day of Resurrection" (*LSB* 478)
  "The Strife Is O'er, the Battle Done" (*LSB* 464)

Easter Sunday

He Is Risen! The Wound of Death Is Vanquished!

Stand

PROCESSIONAL HYMN:
"Awake, My Heart, with Gladness" (*LSB* 467)

INTROIT: Exodus 15:2a, 6, 13, 17–18 (antiphon, Exodus 15:1b)

KYRIE

HYMN OF PRAISE: "This Is the Feast"

SALUTATION AND COLLECT OF THE DAY

Sit

OLD TESTAMENT: Isaiah 25:6–9

GRADUAL: Matthew 28:7; Hebrews 2:7; Psalm 8:6 (adapted)

EPISTLE: 1 Corinthians 5:6b–8

Stand

ALLELUIA VERSE: 2 Timothy 1:10b

HOLY GOSPEL: John 20:1–18

Sit

HYMN OF THE DAY:
"Christ Jesus Lay in Death's Strong Bands" (*LSB* 458)

SERMON:
He Is Risen! The Wound of Death Is Vanquished!
(John 20:11–16)

Stand

Nicene Creed

Prayer of the Church

O Lord Jesus Christ, Sun of Righteousness, You have come forth from the dark night of death, in majesty surpassing the golden Easter dawn. Rise also upon our hearts, and enable us to contemplate the glories of this sacred day, that we may praise and glorify You alone. As our Surety, You were delivered up to death; but, behold, You live. You have conquered death and destroyed him who had the power of death, having bruised the head of the serpent, the ancient foe of God and man. You descended into the lower parts of the earth and spoiled all the principalities and powers, making a show of them openly.

Hail, Lion of the tribe of Judah! O Conqueror of death and Captain of our salvation, the battle and the victory are Yours alone; yet You share Your conquest with us and clothe us with Your triumph. You have become the firstfruits of them that sleep. Because You live, we shall live also. You, the true Paschal Lamb, were offered for us and have taken away the sin of the world. By Your rising again, You have restored to us innocence and everlasting life. Therefore we are glad and rejoice in Your goodness.

O Prince of Life, comfort us with the forgiveness of our sins, and abide with us in steadfast love, that in all our conflicts we may retain the Easter joy. Preserve us in the one true faith; cause us to rise with You in true repentance from our natural death of trespasses and sins and to put away the old leaven of malice and wickedness, that we may always walk with You and serve You in truth and in pureness of living. May Your Spirit put into our minds holy desires and quicken us in all our duties, that through Your power resting upon us we may overcome the world and the terrors of death and at Your coming to judge the world may appear with You in glory, being like You, and having our bodies changed into the fashion of Your own glorious body.

Bless Your inheritance, O Lord; govern Your people; lift them up forever. Defend and maintain Your Church till the end of days. Give us shepherds who take heed to themselves and to the flock; and let all pastors and teachers hold fast the form of sound words of faith and love which are in Christ Jesus.

Into Your hands, O King of kings and Lord of lords, we commit our land and all civil authority everywhere. Endue all rulers and magistrates with wisdom and justice and the fear of Your holy name, and let them punish wickedness and establish peace, that the righteous may flourish and Your name be glorified.

Regard in compassion all who are oppressed by lawless might, all who are suffering for truth and for the sake of conscience, all who are beset with temptations to sin, all who are sinking under the weight of disease, all who are ready to despair of Your grace, all who are troubled by the fear of the grave, all who are entering into the valley of the shadow of death. Be to them the hope of glory, that at Your appearing the trial of their faith may be found to Your praise and honor.

Now to You—the only One able to keep us from falling and able to present us faultless before the presence of Your glory with exceeding joy—to the only wise God, our Savior, be glory and majesty, dominion and power, now and forever.

C: Amen.

Sit

OFFERING

Stand

OFFERTORY: "What Shall I Render to the Lord"

PREFACE

PROPER PREFACE

SANCTUS

PRAYER OF THANKSGIVING

THE WORDS OF OUR LORD

PROCLAMATION OF CHRIST

LORD'S PRAYER

PAX DOMINI

AGNUS DEI

Sit

DISTRIBUTION HYMNS
"Jesus Lives! The Victory's Won" (*LSB* 490)
"Jesus, Grant That Balm and Healing" (*LSB* 421)
"The Head That Once Was Crowned with Thorns" (*LSB* 532)

"At the Lamb's High Feast We Sing" (*LSB* 633)

Stand

Post-Communion Canticle:
"Thank the Lord and Sing His Praise"

Post-Communion Collect

O Lord, in this wondrous Sacrament You have left us a remembrance of Your passion. Grant that we may so receive the sacred mystery of Your body and blood that the fruits of Your redemption may continually be manifested in us; for You live and reign with the Father and the Holy Spirit, one God, now and forever.

Benediction

Closing Hymn: "The Strife Is O'er, the Battle Done" (*LSB* 464)

NOTES ON THE EASTER SERVICE
FOR THE WORSHIP PLANNER

Pastors and congregations certainly do not have to be told the significance of Easter! The following suggestions pertain to the propers of this great high Feast of the Resurrection of Our Lord in continuity with and conclusion of the Lenten series *Sacred Head, Now Wounded*. These suggestions are intended for the Chief Divine Service of Easter Sunday, but they do draw upon the propers otherwise appointed for both the Easter Sunrise and Easter Sunday services. In a congregation where both services will be celebrated, the pastor may want to consider using 1 Corinthians 15:1–11 and Mark 16:1–8 at the Easter Sunday service.

Congregations are likely to have their own established patterns for the selection and use of the various settings of the Divine Service. These recommendations include the use of Setting One or Two of the Divine Service in *Lutheran Service Book* throughout Eastertide. It can be preferable to alternate settings within a congregation by whole seasons of the Church Year. Of course, there are advantages and disadvantages to the use of multiple settings. It can become distracting to the people of God when the ordinary rites of the Divine Service differ, not only according to their musical setting but also in translation. Hence the suggested alternatives to the historic ordinary rites, such as "This Is the Feast" in place of the Gloria in Excelsis, that are provided here. Pastors and worship planners will use discernment in making choices that best serve the Gospel within their own congregations.

The Feast of the Resurrection of Our Lord is, in its entirety, such a proclamation of the Gospel of the forgiveness of sins that beginning the day with the usual rites of preparation (that is, Confession and Absolution) may inadvertently detract from the decidedly evangelical thrust of the entire service. Depending on a variety of local customs and circumstances, therefore, pastors are urged to consider omitting the rites of preparation altogether, moving directly to the altar during the processional hymn and proceeding with the Introit immediately upon the conclusion of the hymn. It may be remembered that the rites of preparation were a late (post-Reformation) addition to the order of the Divine Service and, properly speaking, do not belong to the service itself.

Finally, though it is not indicated in *Lutheran Service Book: Altar Book*, the Collect of the Day for Maundy Thursday, normally ascribed to Thomas Aquinas, has historically been regarded as a suitable Post-Communion Collect. It serves particularly well in that capacity throughout the Easter season, where it has the nice advantage of retaining the unity of the cross and resurrection of our Lord. It also serves well in connection with the emphases of the *Sacred Head, Now Wounded* Lenten series. Thus for that reason its use is recommended.

The color of the day for Easter Sunday is white and/or gold.

- This service is based on Setting One and Two of the Divine Service in *Lutheran Service Book*.

- The hymn suggested for the processional may be used during the distribution of Holy Communion.

- An alternate choice for the processional hymn is "Christ the Lord Is Risen Today; Alleluia" (*LSB* 463)

- The "Song of Moses and Israel" (*LSB* 925) may be used in place of the suggested Introit.

- The Prayer of the Church is adapted from pages 349–50 of *The Lutheran Liturgy*.

- The Post-Communion Collect suggested in this service is the Collect of the Day for Maundy Thursday. Pastoral discretion and local custom will guide the choice of collect.

- Additional hymn choices include:

  "All the Earth with Joy Is Sounding" (*LSB* 462)
  "Baptismal Waters Cover Me" (*LSB* 616)
  "Come, You Faithful, Raise the Strain" (*LSB* 487)
  "Crown Him with Many Crowns" (*LSB* 525)
  "Good Christian Friends, Rejoice and Sing" (*LSB* 475)
  "Hail Thee, Festival Day" (*LSB* 489)
  "He Is Arisen! Glorious Word" (*LSB* 488)
  "How Sweet the Name of Jesus Sounds" (*LSB* 524)
  "I Am Content! My Jesus Ever Lives" (*LSB* 468)
  "If Christ Had Not Been Raised from Death" (*LSB* 486)
  "Jesus Christ, My Sure Defense" (*LSB* 741)
  "Lord, Enthroned in Heavenly Splendor" (*LSB* 534)
  "Lord Jesus Christ, Life-Giving Bread" (*LSB* 625)
  "Now All the Vault of Heaven Resounds" (*LSB* 465)
  "Our Paschal Lamb, That Sets Us Free" (*LSB* 473)
  "Thanks to Thee, O Christ, Victorious" (*LSB* 548)
  "The Day of Resurrection" (*LSB* 478)
  "This Joyful Eastertide" (*LSB* 482)

CHORAL AND INSTRUMENTAL MUSIC RECOMMENDATIONS

The *Sacred Head, Now Wounded* Lenten series provides choirs and vocal ensembles with a wealth of resources that correspond to this hymn and this theme. In the following list, suggestions are made for choral and instrumental settings of the hymn "O Sacred Head, Now Wounded," as well as other corresponding choices.

Choral recommendations are given also for hymn settings for use throughout the Lenten season, as well as music choices for Ash Wednesday and Holy Week. This music would be most appropriate as a response to a Scripture reading or as music during the collection of the offering, during distribution of the Lord's Supper, or even as the prelude to the service. Psalm settings are also provided that would allow the presentation of a choral psalm in the Divine Service, Vespers, or Evening Prayer.

Worship planners and church musicians also will find some recommendations for Easter, especially those pieces that correspond to Christ, our wounded and risen Savior.

All these ideas reinforce the vital role of the choir in the Church and within the liturgy as a servant of the Word. Avoid diminishing the choir's function simply to filling the "anthem slot." As Lent is traditionally a season of teaching the faith (catechesis), choirs and choir directors can use this holy season as an opportunity to learn as well.

Choral and Instrumental Music

Title	Composer	Setting	Vendor & Stock No.	Notes
O Sacred Head, Now Wounded (in *The Parish Choir Book*)	Bach	SATB	CPH 97-7574	
O Sacred Head, Now Wounded	Hoelty-Nickel, ed.	TTBB	CPH 97-7602	
O Sacred Head, Now Wounded	Nelson	SATB, organ, cello	CPH 98-3644	
O Sacred Head, Now Wounded	Reger	SATB, soloists, organ, violin, oboe	CPH 98-3161	A chorale cantata; full score and instrumental parts (CPH 97-6255)

Settings of "Herzlich tut mich verlangen" / "O Sacred Head, Now Wounded" for Organ or Piano and/or Instruments

Composer	Setting	Vendor & Stock No.	Notes	
Leavitt	*A Little Passion Suite for Organ*	CPH 97-6467		
Eithun	*Abide with Us* (piano)	CPH 97-7277		
Callahan	*Chorale Preludes and Postludes for Manuals*, Vol. 1	CPH 97-6874		
Maxwell	*Crucified and Risen Lord*	CPH 97-7281		
Gerike, ed.	*Song of the Gospel*, Vol. 2	CPH 97-7200	Settings by Walther, Brahms, Reger	
Mahnke	*Fourteen Pieces for Treble Instrument and Organ*	CPH 97-6547	C or B-flat instrument	
Herald	*Hymn Arrangements for Instrumental Ensembles*	CPH 97-6263		
Henkelmann	*Instruments for All Seasons*, Vol. 1	CPH 97-7227		
Bennett/Kosnik, ed.	*Laudate!* Vol. 3	CPH 97-6591		
Dengler	*Lenten Piano Variations* (piano)	CPH 97-6705		

Composer	Setting	Vendor & Stock No.	Notes	
Leavitt	*Lenten Reflections for Piano*	CPH 97-6935		
Keesecker	*Piano Impressions for Lent*	CPH 97-6779		
Rinck	*Seven Lenten Pieces* (organ)	CPH 97-6066		
Vandertuin	*Three for Holy Week* (organ)	CPH 97-6993		
Corl	*Three Preludes for the Paschal Season* (organ)	CPH 97-7249		
Sadowski	*Twenty-two Hymn Introductions*	CPH 97-6644		

Psalm Settings

Title	Composer	Setting	Vendor & Stock No.	Notes
Psalm 4 (on CD-ROM *Psallite*)	Gerike	Unison w/congregation	CPH 97-6987	
Create in Me a Clean Heart, O God	Bouman	SA	CPH 98-1143	Psalm 51:10–12
Create in Me a Clean Heart, O God (also in *A Church Choir Book*)	Willan	SATB	CPH 98-2238	Psalm 51:10–12
Create in Me a Clean Heart, O God (in *A Second Morning Star Choir Book*)	Schalk	2-part	CPH 97-4702	Psalm 51:10–12
Create in Me	Roth	unison, 1 or 2 instruments, keyboard	CPH 98-3389	Psalm 51
I Will Give Thanks to the Lord	Cherwien	unison	CPH 98-2930	Psalm 111
Lord, Hear My Prayer	Schütz	2-part, keyboard	CPH 98-3563	Psalm 4:1; 5:2
Lord, Make Me to Know Thy Ways	Byrd/Lovelace	SATB, organ	CPH 98-2935	Psalm 25:4, 5a
My God, Why Dost Thou Now Forsake Me	Callahan	SATB	CPH 98-2975	Psalm 22
Psalm 30 (*Hymnal Supplement 98*)			CPH 97-6686	
From the Depths (*De Profundis*) (in *A First Motet Book*)	Mozart	SATB	CPH 97-4845	Psalm 130
Psalm 130: Out of the Depths	S. Johnson	SATB	CPH 98-3487	

Title	Composer	Setting	Vendor & Stock No.	Notes
Psalm 130	Sadowski	2-part mixed	CPH 98-3058	Optional congregational antiphon
My God, My God, O Lord, My God (in *Ten Psalms from the "Becker Psalter"*)	Schütz	SATB	CPH 97-6303	Paraphrase of Psalm 22

Related Organ, Choral, and Hymn Settings

Title	Composer	Setting	Vendor & Stock No.	Notes
A Lamb Goes Uncomplaining Forth (in *A Third Morning Star Choir Book*)	Micheelsen	unison, organ	CPH 97-4972	
A Lamb Goes Uncomplaining Forth (in *Concordia Classics*)	Wienhorst	SAB	CPH 98-3465	From a reproducible collection
A Lamb Goes Uncomplaining Forth (in *Song of the Gospel*, Vol. 2)	Gerike, ed.	organ settings by Pachelbel, Krapf, Hildebrand	CPH 97-7200	
Be Watchful, Re Ready	Behnke	2-pt. mixed, keyboard, opt. 3 octave handbells	CPH 98-3665	Reflective of Matthew 26:36–46
From Depths of Woe (in *Jubilee*)	Gerike	TTBB	CPH 98-3613	Reproducible collection
From Depths of Woe I Cry to Thee	Heim, ed.	SATB, organ, opt. flute, strings	CPH 98-3879	Settings by Johann Walter and Arnold von Bruck
From Depths of Woe I Cry to Thee (in *Hymn Tune Portraits*)	Nelson	organ	CPH 97-7027	Also in *Song of the Gospel*, Vol. 1 (CPH 97-7202)
From Depths of Woe I Cry to Thee (in *Six Hymn Improvisations*, Vol. 3)	Hildebrand	organ	CPH 97-6938	Also in *Song of the Gospel*, Vol. 1 (CPH 97-7202)
From Depths of Woe I Cry to Thee (*Song of the Gospel*, Vol. 1)	Zachau	organ	CPH 97-7202	
From Depths of Woe (in *Twenty Hymn Introductions*)	Sadowski	organ	CPH 97-6026	

Title	Composer	Setting	Vendor & Stock No.	Notes
If Your Beloved Son, O God (in *Master Organ Works of Jan Bender*, Vol. 4)	Fienen, ed.	organ	CPH 97-7101	
If Your Beloved Son, O God (in *Musica Sacra*, Vol. 2)	Kosche	organ	CPH 97-7015	
If Your Beloved Son, O God (in *Six Hymn Improvisations*, Set 2)	Hildebrand	organ	CPH 97-6886	
If Your Beloved Son, O God (in *Sonus Novus*, Vol. 3)	Loemker	organ	CPH 97-7044	
If Your Beloved Son, O God (in *Song of the Gospel*, Vol. 1)	Gerike, ed.	organ	CPH 97-7202	
In the Midst of Earthly Life (in *The SAB Chorale Book*)	Hennig	SAB	CPH 97-7575	Men have the melody in this setting
In the Shattered Bliss	Text by Starke; setting by Hildebrand	SATB, organ, brass	CPH 98-3741; 97-7037 (full score)	Good for Maundy Thursday, also during Lent
Jesus, I Will Ponder Now	Vieregge	unison or SAB	CPH 98-2916	Concertato
Jesus, Priceless Treasure	Bach/Leavitt	SATB	CPH 98-3908	Could be sung by a quartet instead of a choir
Lamb of God	F. M. Christiansen	SATB	Augsburg Fortress 9780800652593; 9786000175788 (a cappella)	
Lamb of God, Pure and Holy (in *We Praise Thee*, Part I)	Willan	SA	CPH 97-7564	
Lamb of God (in *Bach for All Seasons*)	Bach		Augsburg Fortress 9780800658540	
Lamb of God (in *Unison and Two-part Anthems*)	Pooler		Augsburg Fortress 9780800648916	
Lamb of God, Pure and Holy (in *Eighteen [Leipzig] Chorales*)	J. S. Bach		Breitkopf & other publishers	
Lamb of God, Pure and Holy (in *Neumeister Chorales*)	J. S. Bach		Breitkopf	

Title	Composer	Setting	Vendor & Stock No.	Notes
Lamb of God, Pure and Holy (in *Orgelbüchlein*)	J. S. Bach		CPH 97-5774	
Lamb of God, Pure and Holy (in *Lamb of God: Five Lenten Hymn Settings*)	Cherwien		MorningStar 10-302	
Lamb of God, Pure and Holy (in *Eight Lenten Chorales for Manuals*)	Kickstat		MorningStar 10-307	
Lamb of God, Pure and Holy (in *Choralvorspiele, Vol. 7*)	Max Reger		Breitkopf	
Lamb of God, Pure and Holy (in *Chorale Preludes and Postludes for Manuals, Vol. 3*)	Callahan		CPH 97-6930	
Lamb of God, Pure and Holy (in *Imprint Your Image: Easy Organ Settings for Lent*)	Hildebrand		CPH 97-7207	
Now Let Your Servant	Cherwien	SATB, opt. flute, piano	CPH 98-3482	Choir could prepare this for use with *Lutheran Service Book* (Nunc Dimittis)
O Dearest Jesus, What Law Hast Thou Broken (in *The SAB Chorale Book*)	Metzler	SAB	CPH 97-7575	Men have the melody in this setting
O Dearest Lord, Thy Sacred Head	Johnson	SATB, organ	Augsburg Fortress 978-0-8006-4579-3	An easy setting of an early American folktune; text is reflective of "O Sacred Head"
The St. Matthew Passion	Schuetz/ Rosolack	SATB	GIA Publications G-3721	
The Road to Calvary	Bach/Cozens	SATB	CPH 98-1629	Collection of Bach chorales
What Wondrous Love	Behnke	SATB, opt. congregation, keyboard	CPH 98-3598	
Why Should Cross and Trial Grieve Me (in *Song of the Gospel, Vol. 2*)	Gerike, ed.	organ	CPH 97-7200	Partita by Johann Walther

Ash Wednesday

See settings of Psalm 51 and 130, plus "From Depths of Woe I Cry to Thee" above.

Title	Composer	Setting	Vendor & Stock No.	Notes
Return to the Lord	Kosche	2-part	CPH 98-3798	Joel 2:13, the verse for Ash Wednesday and Lent
Return to the Lord (in *Proclaim the Mercy of Christ*)	Gerike	TTBB	CPH 98-3274	Joel 2:13, the verse for Ash Wednesday and Lent
Return to the Lord Your God	Gerike	SATB	CPH 98-2742	Joel 2:13, the verse for Ash Wednesday and Lent
The Beautiful Treasure	Haan	SATB, kb, fl	CPH 98-3758	Reflects the Ash Wednesday Gospel
Treasures in Heaven	Sadowski	SATB	CPH 98-3753	Reflects the Ash Wednesday Gospel
Treasure in Heaven	Frahm	SAB, kb	CPH 98-3253	Reflects the Ash Wednesday Gospel
Treasure	Graham	SATB, keyboard, cello or bassoon	CPH 98-3541	

Maundy Thursday

Title	Composer	Setting	Vendor & Stock No	Notes
Ave verum corpus	Mozart	SATB	Various editions	
In the Shattered Bliss	Text by Starke; setting by Hildebrand	SATB, organ, brass	CPH 98-3741; 97-7037 (full score)	May also be used throughout Lent
Jesus, Sun of Life, My Splendor	Handel/Bunjes	SATB, organ (opt. strings)	CPH 98-1445	Text is from the hymn "Soul Adorn Thyself with Gladness"
O Lord, We Praise You (in *O Living Bread*)	Hildebrand	organ	CPH 97-7152	

Title	Composer	Setting	Vendor & Stock No.	Notes
O Lord, We Praise You (in *European Connection*, Vol. 1)	Behnke, ed.	organ	CPH 97-6782	
O Lord, We Praise You (in *Six Hymn Improvisations*, Set 1)	Hildebrand	organ	CPH 97-6763	
O Lord, We Praise You (in *Song of the Gospel*, Vol. 1)	Gerike, ed.	organ	CPH 97-7202	
You, Lord, We Praise	Proulx	2-part and 5 handbells	CPH 98-3448	
What Is This Bread?	von Kampen	SATB, SAB, 2-part	CPH 98-3658 (SATB/SAB); 98-3705 (2-part)	

Good Friday

Title	Composer	Setting	Vendor & Stock No.	Notes
The Passion according to St. John	Schalk	SATB and soloists	CPH 97-7258	Very accessible for parish choirs
Behold the Lamb of God (in *The Morning Star Choir Book*)	Bouman	Unison/2-part	CPH 97-6287	John 1:29
Passion according to St. John	Lovelace/Victoria	SATB	CPH 97-5430	Narration may be spoken or chanted
St. John Passion Choruses	Victoria/Rowan	SATB	GIA Publications	
Passion according to St. John	Byrd	SAB	CPH 97-4868	
Passion according to St. John	Hillert	SATB	CPH 97-5209	Accessible for parish choirs with enough rehearsal
The Passion according to St. John	Schuetz	SATB	GIA Publications	
My God, My God, O Lord, My God (in *Ten Psalms from the "Becker Psalter"*)	Schütz	SATB	CPH 97-6303	Paraphrase of Psalm 22
The Blood of Jesus Christ, the Son of God (in *The SAB Choir Goes for Baroque*)	Schütz	SAB	CPH 97-5232	1 John 1:7
Lamentations of Jeremiah	Schalk	SATB	CPH 98-3601	Four short pieces could be sung individually or as a set

Title	Composer	Setting	Vendor & Stock No.	Notes
The Reproaches for Good Friday	Wienhorst	SATB or unison	CPH 98-2871	Could be used throughout Lent
The Road to Calvary	Bach/Cozens	SATB	CPH 98-1629	Collection of Bach chorales
The Seven Words from the Cross	Hillert	SATB, soloists, opt. handbells	CPH 97-7169	

Other Suggestions for throughout Lent

Title	Composer	Setting	Vendor & Stock No.	Notes
Behold the Lamb of God (in *The Morning Star Choir Book*)	Bouman	unison/2-part	CPH 97-6287	John 1:29
Come, Let Us Fix Our Eyes on Jesus	Kosche	2-part; optional instruments	CPH 98-3198	Hebrews 12:2, the Gradual for Lent
Surely He Has Borne Our Griefs	Sadowski	SATB	CPH 98-3650	
Surely He Has Borne Our Griefs (in *A First Motet Book*)	Hillert	SATB	CPH 97-4845	Isaiah 53:4
Surely He Hath Borne Our Griefs (in *We Praise Thee*, Part II)	Willan	2-part, organ	No longer in print.	Isaiah 53:4
The Blood of Jesus Christ, the Son of God (in *The SAB Choir Goes for Baroque*)	Schütz	SAB	CPH 97-5232	1 John 1:7
Holy Cross of Jesus	Text by Starke; setting by Busarow	SATB, organ, trumpet	CPH 98-3751	Speaks of Suffering Servant, links to Baptism
Lamentations of Jeremiah	Schalk	SATB	CPH 98-3601	Four short pieces could be sung individually or as a set
The Reproaches for Good Friday	Wienhorst	SATB or unison	CPH 98-2871	
The Road to Calvary	Bach/Cozens	SATB	CPH 98-1629	Collection of Bach chorales

Easter

Title	Composer	Setting	Vendor & Stock No.	Notes
Alleluia! For Christ the Lord Is Risen	Bach/Leavitt	2-part or unison and keyboard	CPH 98-3710	
And Sleeps My Lord in Silence Yet	Music	SATB, organ, flute	CPH 98-3845	Especially effective for the Easter Vigil before the Hymn of Praise
At the Lamb's High Feast We Sing	Cherwien	SATB, trumpet, timpani	CPH 98-2864	Concertato
Be Known to Us, Lord Jesus	Schalk	SATB, organ, brass quartet, timpani, congregation	CPH 98-3202; 97-6485 (full score)	
Christ Jesus Lay in Death's Strong Bands	Hildebrand	SATB, organ, brass, timpani, congregation	CPH 97-7111	Available as reproducible score
I Am the Resurrection and the Life	Croft	SATB, opt. keyboard	CPH 98-3747	John 11:25–26; Job 19:25–27; 1:21 (KJV)
The Paschal Lamb Who Suffered for Us	Schalk	SATB, div.	CPH 98-3316	
This Joyful Eastertide	Wood/Leavitt	SATB	CPH 98-3744	
Worthy Is Christ	Hillert	Soprano descant along with instrumental parts	CPH 98-2305	If your choir has sopranos that can handle descants, it's easy to add this descant to the congregational canticle from *LSB* Divine Service, Setting One